Win
BIGLY

Win BIGLY

PERSUASION IN A WORLD WHERE FACTS DON'T MATTER

SCOTT ADAMS

PORTFOLIO/PENGUIN

Portfolio/Penguin
An imprint of Penguin Random House LLC
375 Hudson Street
New York, New York 10014

Most Portfolio books are available at a discount when purchased in quantity for sales promotions or corporate use. Special editions, which include personalized covers, excerpts, and corporate imprints, can be created when purchased in large quantities. For more information, please call (212) 572-2232 or e-mail specialmarkets@penguinrandomhouse.com. Your local bookstore can also assist with discounted bulk purchases using the Penguin Random House corporate Business-to-Business program. For assistance in locating a participating retailer, e-mail B2B@penguinrandomhouse.com.

Library of Congress Cataloging-in-Publication Data

Names: Adams, Scott, 1957– author.
Title: Win bigly : persuasion in a world where facts don't matter / Scott Adams.
Description: New York : Portfolio HC, 2017.
Identifiers: LCCN 2017034760 | ISBN 9780735219717 (hardcover) |
ISBN 9780735219724 (e-book) | ISBN 9780525533320 (international export edition)
Subjects: LCSH: Persuasion (Psychology) | Blogs—United States. | Deception—United States. | Truthfulness and falsehood—United States. | Social psychology—United States. | Trump, Donald, 1946–
Classification: LCC BF637.P4 A23 2017 | DDC 303.3/42–dc23 LC record available at https://lccn.loc.gov/2017034760

Printed in the United States of America
1 3 5 7 9 10 8 6 4 2

Penguin is committed to publishing works of quality and integrity. In that spirit, we are proud to offer this book to our readers; however, the story, the experiences, and the words are the author's alone.

This publication is designed to provide accurate and authoritative information in regard to the subject matter covered. It is sold with the understanding that the publisher is not engaged in rendering legal, accounting, or other professional services. If you require legal advice or other expert assistance, you should seek the services of a competent professional.

While the author has made every effort to provide accurate telephone numbers, Internet addresses, and other contact information at the time of publication, neither the publisher nor the author assumes any responsibility for errors or for changes that occur after publication. Further, the publisher does not have any control over and does not assume any responsibility for author or third-party Web sites or their content.

For Kristina, my love and my muse

CONTENTS

PART 3

HOW PRESIDENT TRUMP DOES WHAT OTHERS CAN'T

PART 4

HOW TO USE PERSUASION IN BUSINESS AND POLITICS

PART 5
WHY JOINING A TRIBE MAKES YOU POWERFUL
AND BLIND

PREAMBLE: THE DAY MY REALITY SPLIT INTO TWO

In February of 2016 I began to experience two separate realities at the same time.

In one reality, candidate for president Donald Trump had just ended his chances of becoming president of the United States by refusing to disavow the KKK, and David Duke, on a CNN interview with Jake Tapper. Trump said he didn't hear the question.

This was a big problem for candidate Trump. It was also a big problem for me. I was one of the earliest public figures to have predicted Trump's win, and I was in the middle of an unplanned career pivot from "guy who created the *Dilbert* comic" to something like a political pundit. My blog traffic went through the roof whenever I wrote about Trump's skill as a persuader. I don't know much about politics, but I know skillful persuasion when I see it. As it turned out, there was a big demand for what I called my "persuasion filter" on the race. Producers for news outlets both large and small were scrambling to get me on their shows.

I wrote and spoke so much about Trump's persuasion skills that people labeled me a Trump supporter, although not in the sense of supporting his policies. By then my writing about Trump had already cost me half of my friends. My lucrative speaking career had dropped to zero, and I didn't expect any new *Dilbert* licensing deals. I had become toxic for any kind of mixed crowd. But I was okay with my situation because I expected to be right in my prediction that Trump would win it all. Winning fixes most problems.

Although the polls disagreed with me, I thought my prediction of a Trump win was looking good until the Jake Tapper interview on CNN. In this version of reality, I had foolishly alienated my friends, annihilated my professional reputation, and cut my income in half. And all I would get in return was a *Wikipedia* entry under my name saying I had supported an alleged racist for president. The situation was less than ideal.

I publicly disavowed Trump because of his CNN interview, just to get out of the blast zone. But by then it was too late to salvage everything I had already lost. Like an idiot, I had managed to turn a respected career as one of the top cartoonists in the country into a grimy embarrassment that wouldn't wash off.

That was one version of reality.

I experienced a second version of reality at the same time. This version involved Trump brushing off the CNN/KKK controversy and going on to win the presidency. In that version of reality I would be redeemed in the end, at least in terms of being a credible political observer. Winning always feels good.

For the next several months I lived both realities. But I trusted only one of them. I doubled down on my prediction of a Trump win. If that sounds crazy to you, well, that's nothing. We're just getting started. There's plenty more crazy in this book.

Win
BIGLY

INTRODUCTION
(WHERE I PRIME YOU
FOR THE REST)

'm a trained hypnotist.

And I'm going to tell you about the spookiest year of my life. It happened between June 2015 and November 2016. Okay, that's a little more than a year.

Everything you are about to read in this book is true, as far as I know. I don't expect you to believe *all* of it. (Who could?) But I promise it is true, to the best of my knowledge.

I've waited decades to deliver the message in this book. I waited because the world wasn't ready, but also because the messenger—yours truly—didn't have the skill to deliver it right. The story was too hard to tell. But it was important, and it needed to be told.

And so I waited.

And I learned.

And I practiced.

And I waited some more.

Then it happened.

On June 16, 2015, Donald J. Trump rode a golden elevator in Trump Tower to the lobby, where he announced his candidacy for president of the United States. Like most observers at the time, I didn't fully understand what I was seeing. It wasn't until the first Republican primary debate that I realized what was happening right before our eyes. Trump was no ordinary politician. He was no ordinary businessperson either. In fact, he wasn't ordinary in *any* sense of the word.

Trump is what I call a **Master Persuader**. That means he has weapons-grade persuasion skills. Based on my background in that field, I recognized his talents early. And after watching him in action during the election, I have to say that Trump is the most persuasive human I have ever observed.

President Trump carried those persuasion skills into the White House, where his supporters say he has gotten a lot done, and his critics say he hasn't. Supporters pointed to a decrease in illegal immigration, a strong stock market (at this writing), high consumer confidence, progress fighting ISIS, a solid Supreme Court nominee, and a stronger-than-expected foreign policy game. Critics saw "chaos" in the administration, slow progress on health-care reform, and maybe some kind of nefarious connections with Russia.

President Trump's critics (and mine) asked me how I could call the president a Master Persuader when his public approval levels were in the cellar. The quick answer is that low approval didn't stop him from winning the presidency. And according to his supporters, it didn't stop him from getting things done on the job. His persuasion skills, combined with the power of the presidency, were all he needed. Keep in mind that disapproving of Trump's style and personality is a social requirement for people who long for a more civil world. Effectiveness is a separate issue from persuasive skill.

But here's the fun part: I also believed that Trump—the Master Persuader—was going to do far more than win the presidency. I expected Trump to rip a hole in the fabric of reality so we could look through it to a deeper truth about the human experience. And he did exactly that.

But not everyone noticed. That's why I made it the theme of this book.

The common worldview, shared by most humans, is that there is one objective reality, and we humans can understand that reality through a rigorous application of facts and reason. This view of the world imagines that some people have already achieved a fact-based type of enlightenment that is compatible with science and logic, and they are trying to help the rest of us see the world the "right" way. As far as I can tell, most people share that interpretation of the world. The only wrinkle with that world-view is that we all think we are the enlightened ones. And we assume the people who disagree with us just need better facts, and perhaps better brains, in order to agree with us. That filter on life makes most of us happy—because we see ourselves as the smart ones—and it does a good job of predicting the future, but only because confirmation bias (our tendency to interpret data as supporting our views) will make the future look any way we want it to look, *within reason.*

What I saw with Trump's candidacy for president is that the "within reason" part of our understanding about reality was about to change, bigly. I knew that candidate Trump's persuasion skills were about to annihilate the public's ability to understand what they were seeing, because their observations wouldn't fit their mental model of living in a rational world. The public was about to transition from believing—with total certainty—"the clown can't win" to "Hello, President Trump." And in order to make that transition, they would have to rewrite every movie playing in their heads. To put it in simple terms, the only way Trump could win was if everything his critics understood about the true nature of reality was wrong.

Then Trump won.

That's what I mean by "ripping a hole in the fabric of the universe." Think of it as the moment your entire worldview dissolves in front of your eyes, and you have to rebuild it from scratch. As a trained persuader, I found this situation thrilling beyond words. And I was about to get a lot of company, once people realized what they were seeing.

I'll help you find the hole that Trump punched through the universe so you can look through it with me to the other side. Put a seat belt on your brain—you're going to need it.

Before we go further, I need to tell you that Trump's stated policies during the campaign did not align with my political preferences. Nor do my views line up with Clinton's stated policies during the race. I realize this is hard to believe, so I'll need to give you some examples to make the point. This little detour is necessary so you can judge my political bias.

It is important context because the message is always connected to the messenger. If you are a regular reader of my blog, you can probably skip this part.

I label myself an ultraliberal, and by that I mean liberals seem too conservative to me. I'll give you some examples:

- Generally speaking, conservatives want to ban abortion while liberals want it to remain legal. I go one step further and say that men should sideline themselves from the question and follow the lead of women on the topic of reproductive health. (Men should still be in the conversation about their own money, of course.) Women take on most of the burden of human reproduction, including all of the workplace bias, and that includes even the women who don't plan to have kids. My personal sense of ethics says that the people who take the most responsibility for important societal outcomes should also have the strongest say. My male opinion on women's reproductive health options adds nothing to the quality of the decision. Women have it covered. The most credible laws on abortion are the ones that most *women* support. And when life-and-death issues are on the table, credibility is essential to the smooth operation of society. My opinion doesn't add credibility to the system. When I'm not useful, I like to stay out of the way.

- Generally speaking, conservatives are opposed to legalization of marijuana whereas liberals are more likely to support it. I go one step further and suggest that doctors prescribe recreational drugs for old people to make their final years enjoyable. What do they have to lose? (Yes, I'm serious. I know it's hard to tell.)

- When it comes to complicated issues about economics and foreign affairs, my opinion is that I never have enough data to form competent opinions. Neither does anyone else. My opinion of my own limitations doesn't match that of any politician. They pretend they have enough information to make informed decisions.

• Generally speaking, conservatives think we live in a country where everyone already has equal opportunity. Liberals generally think the government should do more to guarantee equal opportunity. I go one step further and suggest considering slavery reparations for African Americans in the form of free college and job training, funded by a twenty-five-year tax on the top 1 percent. In the long run, I want free education for all, but you have to start someplace. No matter who goes first, it will seem unfair to everyone else. So why not let African Americans in low-income families go first? Keep in mind that helping the demographic group that is in the deepest hole gives society the biggest economic bang for the buck. And when society is prosperous, most of it flows right back into the pockets of the 1 percent, making their taxes for this purpose almost an investment.

I hope those are enough examples to make my point. I'm not on any political team, and I like it that way.

Policies aside, I was clearly a Trump "supporter" in the sense that I spoke glowingly of his persuasion skills, his humor, and his business talent. I was among the first observers—some say the first—to identify his political maneuvering as solid strategies borrowed from the business world. I was making that point while most pundits were labeling him an unhinged clown. I know a lot about business because I've observed it, and lived it, in a lot of ways. I write about business in the *Dilbert* comic, and I've published several business humor books. I also spent sixteen years in corporate America, first at a large bank and later at a phone company. I held about a dozen different jobs at those companies and got to see business from the perspective of technologists, marketers, strategists, leaders, followers, and more. I also have a BA in economics and an MBA from the Haas School of Business at UC Berkeley. And I've managed several different types of businesses of my own. The *Dilbert* business is a substantial enterprise, and I manage that. I also cofounded a start-up called

PERSUASION TIP 1

When you identify as part of a group, your opinions tend to be biased toward the group consensus.

WhenHub, and I help manage that. I make no claim of being a great businessperson, but I can usually tell the difference between good business practices and bad. Political pundits and writers covering Trump during the campaign generally did not have business experience, and I think that put them at a huge disadvantage in understanding the power of his methods. It wasn't all about persuasion. He also used high-end business strategy all the way, and you wouldn't recognize it as such if you had never spent time in that world.

As I grew my number of social media followers by attracting Trump supporters, it was fun to play to the audience. They liked pro-Trump humor and content and I enjoyed delivering it. The funniest observers of the election seemed to be on the political right. I'm attracted to funny.

I did sometimes criticize Trump, and I sometimes praised Clinton when her persuasion game was good. But I made no attempt at balancing the two for the sake of appearances. The mainstream media was doing a good job of covering all of the candidates' flaws and features. My primary interest was the topic of persuasion. And on that dimension, Trump owned the election until the summer of 2016. That's when Clinton's persuasion game went weapons grade and it became a fair fight for the first time.

If you would like to see my list of Trump's mistakes, I've organized them in appendix D. I did that so you won't think I'm blind to his missteps.

This is a good place to tell you where my credentials rank in the field of persuasion. I label my persuasion skills *commercial grade*, meaning I successfully use persuasion in my work. A few levels above me in talent and credibility are cognitive scientists who study this sort of thing for a living. If a cognitive scientist tells you I got something wrong in this book, trust the scientist, not me.

In my view of the world, the few individuals I call Master Persuaders are a level above cognitive scientists in persuasion power and possess what I call weapons-grade persuasion skills. The qualities that distinguish weapons-grade persuasion from the academic or commercial types are the level of risk taking and the personality that goes with it. Trump the candidate had an appetite for risk, a deep understanding of persuasion, and a personality that the media couldn't ignore. He brought the full package.

Here's the summary of the persuader types. The most powerful are at the top.

- Master Persuaders (includes several presidents, Steve Jobs, Peggy Noonan, Tony Robbins, Madonna, etc.)
- Cognitive scientists
- Commercial-grade persuaders (people such as me)

I'll try to compensate for my lack of a PhD in cognitive science by linking to sources where it makes sense. But much of this book is based on decades of personal practice and observation of what works and what doesn't in the realm of persuasion. *I encourage readers to remain skeptical and to check any of my claims on their own.* A simple Google search will confirm (or debunk?) almost anything I say in this book about persuasion.

BUT SCOTT, TRUMP IS A HORRIBLE MONSTER, ISN'T HE?

Trump's critics were appalled that I could say anything positive about this horrible monster that they expected to sprout horns at any moment. To them, my so-called support of Trump represented a big risk for the country, and it was the most despicable thing I could do. They worried that my writing would help get this racist, sexist, disrespectful, xenophobic hater elected. And they asked me how I could live with myself as Hitler's Little Helper. Wasn't I taking a risk with the future of the entire planet? Was I putting everyone's life in danger just to have some fun and get some attention?

The simple answer is that I didn't see any of their concerns as real. In Trump I saw a highly capable yet flawed man trying to make a positive difference. And I saw all of his opponents' fears as the product of heavy-handed political persuasion. No one becomes Hitler at age seventy. We would have seen lots of warning signs during his decades of public life.

And I kept in mind that most Republican candidates for president have been painted with the same Hitler brush, and it hasn't been right yet. In a similar fashion, I knew President Obama was not part of an Islamic terrorist sleeper cell, as some of his critics claimed. I saw candidate Trump as the target of the same sort of partisan hysteria. Like much of the public, I saw a scary extremism in Trump's language and policy preferences during the campaign. But I recognized his hyperbole as weapons-grade persuasion that would change after the election, not a sign that Trump had suddenly turned into Hitler.

When Trump said he would deport millions of undocumented immigrants who were otherwise obeying the law, his critics saw it as the beginning of a Hitler-like roundup of the people who are "different" in some way. I saw it as a thoroughly impractical idea that served as a mental "anchor" to brand Trump as the candidate who cared the most about our porous borders and planned to do the most about them. Never mind that his initial deportation plan was mean, impractical, and—many would say—immoral. Trump's position gave him plenty of room to negotiate back to something more reasonable after he was in office. That's exactly what happened, even if you don't like where he ended up. As I write this, President Trump's current immigration policy is focused on deporting undocumented immigrants who committed serious crimes after entering. His critics probably felt relieved because his opening offer (mass deportation) was so aggressive that his current policy seems more reasonable than it might have without the opening offer for contrast. That is classic deal making. You start with a big first demand and negotiate back to your side of the middle.

When candidate Trump answered questions about policies, it was clear he didn't have a detailed understanding of the more complicated issues. Most observers saw this as a fatal flaw that would keep him out of the White House. I didn't see it that way. I saw it as Trump recognizing that people don't use facts and reason to make decisions. A skilled persuader can blatantly ignore facts and policy details so long as the persuasion is skillful. Candidate Trump matched the emotional state of his base, and matched their priorities too. His supporters trusted him to dig into the details once elected, with the help of advisers and experts. And that's what happened.

I was far from being a true believer about Trump's policies. But unlike most of the world, I recognized his campaign promises as more persuasion than policy. I never took his policy positions too seriously except in a directional sense. And directionally, Trump wanted the same things the public wanted: strong national security, prosperity, affordable health care, personal freedom, and that sort of thing. Although Trump never said it directly, he branded himself as a flexible leader who would work out the details after election. And sure enough, we observed President Trump working out the details after election on immigration policy, health care, taxes, fighting ISIS, and more.

President Trump's policy evolution was generally in the service of moving toward the political middle, as presidents generally do, creating haters on the right as well as the left. My point is that I wasn't invested in Trump's stated policies because I assumed he would drift toward the acceptable middle once he was elected. And that's what we saw. He backed off on mass deportation of undocumented immigrants, waterboarding terrorists, killing the families of terrorists, and calling China a currency manipulator. He educated himself enough on climate change to decide that the Paris climate accord was a bad agreement no matter what anyone thought of the science. On social issues, Trump favored leaving those decisions with the individual states, which is a Republican form of moderation even if you don't like the outcome.

People have asked if I was really as confident in Trump's win as I claimed I was. The answer is that I *did* feel confident in my prediction, to such a degree that it seemed puzzling even to me. I had lots of reasons for my prediction, as you will see throughout the book. But those reasons were not enough to justify my oversized confidence that Trump would win. Clearly there were some irrational processes going on in my mind that made me confident in an outcome that no rational person should have been confident about. I describe some of those influences in the last part of the book. The short version is that I was detecting patterns that all pointed in the same direction. But all of that could have been confirmation bias or magical thinking.

There were a few times during the campaign—usually after Trump did something spectacularly provocative—where my confidence was challenged. In every case, my confidence bounced back quickly, with one exception: the *Access Hollywood* "Pussygate" tapes, in which Trump was caught saying shocking things about his experiences with women. For several days I thought that scandal would be the end of Trump. But even that wasn't enough to keep my irrational confidence in a Trump win from returning. You'll read more about this later in the book.

I made a point of sampling the election news on both sides of the political spectrum. I'm not sure how common that practice is. Most people are habit bound to the news sources that tend to agree with them. The voters who were consuming only left-leaning news were convinced Trump was a monster. The voters consuming conservative news were convinced that Hillary Clinton was evil incarnate.

If you don't sample the news on both sides, you miss a lot of the context. For example, when candidate Trump allegedly mocked a writer with a bad arm, the anti-Trump press played the video on loop to portray Trump as a bad person. But over at the conservative news sites, and on Twitter, you could see older videos of Trump using the same mocking hand gestures in other situations. Apparently he routinely makes the same "spastic" impression when mocking the opinions of his critics. If you watched only liberal-leaning news, you processed that situation as Trump mocking a disabled guy for his disability. *That monster!* But conservatives saw the context, understood the mocking as being generic, and correctly labeled it as so-called fake news. I saw the news coverage on both sides, so I wasn't worried we might elect a president who mocks people's disabilities. When Trump's critics accused him of laziness, ignorance, and cruel intentions, I saw a skilled persuader who knew what mattered and what didn't. Apparently he was more right than wrong on his priorities, because he won the election.

Had I seen signs that the worst accusations against Trump were even

1 percent likely to be true, I would have backed off my support. But as a trained persuader, I saw the scariest accusations against Trump as routine political persuasion, not an indication that Hitler was coming. I never had a moment of doubt on this point. Based on my lifetime of experience with persuasion, the situation was both simple and clear: *It only looked risky to the untrained.*

WHY I COULD SEE (AND SAY) WHAT OTHER PUNDITS COULD NOT

I had an advantage in explaining Trump to the public because I have an unusual talent stack. For starters, I'm a trained hypnotist and a lifelong student of persuasion. Trained persuaders recognize the techniques used by other persuaders in a way that the untrained do not. So I had that going for me.

As I mentioned, I was also among the first (or the first) to point out that Trump was using high-end business strategy that looked crazy to political pundits who had no business experience. I have extensive business experience across a variety of fields, so most of what Trump was doing looked familiar to me. For example, where others saw Trump pushing outrageously impractical and even immoral policies, I saw him using standard negotiating tactics and hyperbole to make it easier to find the middle ground later. And he did.

Like Trump, I grew up in New York State. That helped me understand his communication style. The provocative things Trump said during the campaign shocked much of the country. But to New Yorkers such as me, talking in a way that sounds unnecessarily provocative—as Trump often did during the campaign—is what New Yorkers call "talking." My claim is that it is easier for a New Yorker to understand another New Yorker than it is for a Californian to understand a New Yorker.

I had a lot of advantages in understanding Trump's communication style and his powers of persuasion. But when it came to communicating what I knew, I had one enormous advantage that almost no one else covering the election had: *I wasn't doing it for the money.*

I'm already rich. No one owns me. The common business term for that situation is *having F-you money.* And I have it. That gave me the freedom to say whatever I thought was both useful and true. And thanks to my popular blog at Dilbert.com, I had a direct channel to the public.

I also knew there would be plenty of haters coming at me as soon as I started saying good things about Trump's talents. And come after me they did—amateurs, professionals, and paid trolls alike. Luckily for me, I had a three-word philosophy beginning with *F* and ending with "money" that covered that situation. And I made sure my readers knew that's how I was thinking. The freedom to say whatever I wanted to say—and to do it publicly—was half the fun.

Oh, I also have one more thing going for me: I don't feel shame or embarrassment like normal people. I wasn't always this way. It's a learned skill. And I knew it would take all of my embarrassment-avoidance talents to survive what I expected would be a year of abuse at best, and at worst— if my critics were right—a lifetime of mockery for the things I was about to say in public.

That kind of risk has never stopped me from doing anything. I confess to enjoying the adrenaline of it all. I invite you to come along for the ride in the form of this book. You're going to like it.

I invite people of all political perspectives to enjoy this book without getting sidetracked by politics. I won't be discussing policies except in the context of persuasion. This book isn't designed to change your mind about politics or about Trump. All I hope to do is teach you some things about persuasion by wrapping it in an entertaining first-person story.

With your permission, let's do that.

PART 1

WHY FACTS ARE OVERRATED

THE MOST IMPORTANT
PERCEPTUAL SHIFT
IN HISTORY

My spooky year was fun for me, but it was also a dangerous time for the world's collective mental health. Enlightenment can be risky business. When your old worldview falls apart, it can trigger all kinds of irrational behavior before your brain rewrites the movie in your head to make it consistent with your new worldview. We all have movies in our heads that we believe are accurate views of reality. And those movies are very different. Normally we don't notice the differences in our personal movies, or we don't care. But when politics are involved, the stakes are higher. Then we notice.

Emotions are already raw in election years, and millions of people are focused on the same topics at the same time. That's a barrel of gasoline and a lot of matches in one place. The last thing the country needed was millions of people simultaneously going nuts. I hoped I could reduce that risk by writing about Trump's persuasion talents and preparing the public for what I saw coming.

That will all make more sense later.

I also wanted to make sure the public did not miss the greatest show in the world by looking through the wrong filter. If you watched the entire election cycle and concluded that Trump was nothing but a lucky clown, you missed one of the most important perceptual shifts in the history of humankind. I'll fix that for you in this book.

I knew from my own experience as a hypnotist that Trump's extraordinary skill at persuasion would trigger massive *cognitive dissonance* and plenty of *confirmation bias.* If you're not familiar with those terms, I include quick definitions below. I'll go into more detail later. If you seek enlightenment, these are two of the most important concepts you will ever learn.

Cognitive Dissonance

• This is a mental condition in which people rationalize why their actions are inconsistent with their thoughts and beliefs. For example, if you think you are smart, but you notice yourself doing something that is clearly dumb, you might spontaneously hallucinate that there was actually a good reason for it. Or perhaps you believe you are an honest person, but you observe yourself doing something dishonest. Your brain will instantly generate a delusion to rationalize the discrepancy. This is a common phenomenon in all normal humans, but we generally believe it applies only to *other* people.

Confirmation Bias

• This is the human tendency to see all evidence as supporting your beliefs, even if the evidence is nothing more than coincidence. This is another common phenomenon that we believe happens only to other people.

I saw in the election of 2016 a dangerous situation forming. If the public misunderstood Trump's methods and intentions—and that seemed likely—things could turn ugly. Worse yet, the public might not appreciate the extraordinary richness of their choice in the election. No matter what you thought of Trump or his policies, he certainly was *different.* And he certainly knew how to make things happen. I thought the public deserved to see the Trump candidacy as clearly as possible, without the biased framing that his adversaries were applying.

You might be wondering how confident I was about my prediction that Trump would win. Well, no one is psychic. I can't know with total certainty what the future holds. For example, I couldn't predict what types of scandals would pop up along the way. But I do know persuasion. I know its power in a way that few people do. And I recognized that with Trump's level of persuasion skill, *he was bringing a flamethrower to a stick fight.*

And the poor little sticks didn't see it coming.

I had high confidence that Trump would surprise the pundits and win the election. But he did far more than that. Before the Master Persuader was done with the election, he would also remake the Republican Party in his own image, eviscerate the mainstream media's credibility, and leave the Democratic Party in ruins. The Clinton and Bush dynasties would be charred wrecks on the sides of the road.

Over the course of my writing career, I've made lots of other public predictions. For example, in my 2004 book, *The Religion War,* I predicted the rise of an Islamic caliphate in the Middle East, and their use of hobby-sized drones for terror attacks. That happens to be a good description of ISIS in 2017. I had similar confidence in that prediction as I did in Trump's win.

But I have lots of other predictions in my portfolio that were less accurate. Some were whimsical, or wishful thinking, or run-of-the-mill guessing based on limited data. My Trump predictions were the first ones that used the Master Persuader framing. That's because Master Persuaders are rare.

In the investment realm, I made a small fortune betting on Master Persuader Steve Jobs turning Apple into the company it is today. That worked out for me. Likewise, Master Persuaders Warren Buffett and Charlie Munger made a tidy profit for me when I owned Berkshire Hathaway stock.

You should never take financial advice from cartoonists, but let me tell you one thing that feels safe to share: If the CEO of a publicly traded company is routinely described as having a "reality distortion field"—as was the case with Steve Jobs—keep an eye on that company. That's a sign of a Master Persuader.

For over a year I did numerous TV, radio, podcast, and print interviews on the topic of my blogging that Trump would win in a "land-slide." It was the spookiest, coolest, most fun year of my life. I'm delighted that you are letting me share this story with you. It's a good story. And I'll teach you some insanely useful stuff along the way.

The book is organized by three major themes. We'll start by talking about the limits of the human brain to perceive reality, and that will prime you for the persuasion lessons that follow. Once you have a working understanding of the basics, I'll show you how I used my understanding of persuasion to predict events in the presidential election of 2016.

Keep in mind that the topic of this book is persuasion, and in that realm, President Trump does far more right than wrong. For completeness, appendix D is my discussion of the things candidate Trump did *wrong*. I hope that acknowledgment frees your mind to enjoy the ride.

Ready?

Let's go.

ABOUT FACTS

On August 13, 2015, I predicted in my blog that Donald Trump had a 98 percent chance of winning the presidency *based on his persuasion skills.* A week earlier, the most respected political forecaster in the United States—Nate Silver—had put Trump's odds of winning the Republican nomination at 2 percent in his FiveThirtyEight.com blog.[1] In those early days of the election, the overwhelming majority of pundits in the business regarded Trump as a novelty and a sideshow.

Persuasion is all about the tools and techniques of changing people's minds, with or without facts and reason. When I started writing favorable blog posts about Trump's persuasion talents, it felt like going to war alone. In California, where I live, it seemed as if most Trump supporters were in hiding because of the social and career risks of publicly supporting him. I wasn't counting on anyone's having my back in this fight.

Luckily, I was wrong. Trump's Twitter followers adopted me immediately and had my back every step of the way. When the critics came after me on Twitter and elsewhere, Trump supporters flooded in to back me. I didn't ask them to do it. They just did. One of my motivations for writing this book is that so many people who supported me on Twitter

Some of the rare and notable predictors of Trump's win included Mike Cernovich, Ann Coulter, Stefan Molyneux, Milo Yiannopoulos, Bill Mitchell, Robert Baillieul, John McLaughlin, Allan Lichtman, Nigel Farage, Piers Morgan, and late-to-the-party Michael Moore.

PERSUASION TIP 2

Humans are hardwired to reciprocate favors. If you want someone's cooperation in the future, do something for that person today.

PERSUASION TIP 3

Persuasion is effective even when the subject recognizes the technique. Everyone knows that stores list prices at $9.99 because $10.00 sounds like too much. It still works.

specifically asked me to write it. This book is a favor returned.

By the way, reciprocity is a big thing in persuasion. When you do someone a favor, it triggers an automatic reciprocity reflex in the recipient. Humans are hardwired to reciprocate kindness. Sales professionals use this persuasion method all the time. If a salesperson buys you lunch or fixes a problem for you, you're being persuaded.

You might think you can resist persuasion techniques just by recognizing them in action. But knowing the technique won't protect you as much as you might think. See Persuasion Tip 3.

So why did I say Trump had exactly a 98 percent chance of winning when I couldn't possibly know the odds? That's a persuasion technique. You saw Trump use the intentional wrongness persuasion play over and over, and almost always to good effect. The method goes like this:

1. Make a claim that is *directionally* accurate but has a big exaggeration or factual error in it.
2. Wait for people to notice the exaggeration or error and spend endless hours talking about how wrong it is.
3. When you dedicate focus and energy to an idea, you remember it. And the things that have the most mental impact on you will irrationally seem as though they are high in priority, even if they are not. That's persuasion.

If I had boringly predicted that Trump would win the election, without any odds attached to it, the public would have easily shrugged it off as another minor celebrity's irrelevant opinion. But if I make you pause to argue with me in your mind about the accuracy of the 98 percent estimate, it deepens my persuasion on the main point—that Trump has a surprisingly high likelihood of winning.

I picked 98 percent as my Trump prediction because Nate Silver of FiveThirtyEight.com was saying 2 percent. I did that for branding and persuasion purposes. It is easier to remember my prediction both because of the way it fits with Silver's prediction and for its audacity, which people perceived as "wrongness." The prediction was designed to attract attention, and it did. It was also designed to pair my name with Nate Silver's name to raise my profile by association. That worked too. Social media folks mentioned me in the same sentence with Silver countless times during the election, exactly as I had hoped. And every mention raised my importance as a political observer because I was being compared with someone already important in that field. Keep in mind that at this point in our story I was playing the wrong sport. I was a cartoonist writing about politics and persuasion. I needed whatever credibility I could get to build an audience for my Trump blogging. Using a little bit of wrongness (my precise 98 percent prediction), I managed to attract more attention than I would have otherwise. And that conferred on me some credibility by association. As long as I was literally in the same sentence with Nate Silver, I would gain some credibility by proximity alone.

Trump used the intentional wrongness persuasion play often, and it seemed to work every time, at least in terms of attracting attention where he wanted it. It even works when you know he's doing it. If you're talking about whatever topic he wants you to focus on, he has your mind right where he wants it, even if you are criticizing him for his errors while you are there.

For example, take Trump's campaign promise that he would build a "wall" on the border of Mexico. Common sense tells you that solid walls are not the best solution for all types of terrain. In many locations, the most cost-effective solutions might include wire fences, or digital monitoring of various types, or something else. If Trump had wanted to be accurate, he would have mentioned all of those solutions every time he talked about border security. He did make some casual admissions that the border would be secured in different ways in different places. But most of the time he ignored those details, and wisely so. By continuing to call it a "wall" without details, he caused the public and the media to view that as an error. So they argued about it. They fact-checked it. They put together cost estimates. They criticized Trump for not understanding that it couldn't be a "wall" the entire way. *How stupid can he be?????*

PERSUASION TIP 4

The things that you think about the most will irrationally rise in importance in your mind.

And when they were done criticizing Trump for the "error" of saying he would build one big solid "wall," the critics had convinced themselves that border security was a higher priority than they had thought coming into the conversation. The ideas that you think about the most are the ones that automatically and *irrationally* rise in your mental list of priorities. And Trump made us think about the wall a lot. He did that because he knew voters would see him as the strongest voice on the topic. It also sucked up media energy that might have focused on political topics he didn't understand at the same depth as his competitors. Master Persuaders move your *energy* to the topics that help them, independent of facts and reason.

I've said Trump is the best persuader I have ever seen in action. The wall is a perfect example. Consider how much discipline it took for him to *avoid* continually clarifying that his "wall" was really a patchwork of solutions that depend on the terrain. In order to pull off this type of weapons-grade persuasion, he had to be willing to endure brutal criticism about how dumb he was to think he could secure the border with a solid wall. To make those criticisms go away, all Trump needed to do was clarify that the "wall" was actually a variety of different border solutions, depending on cost and terrain, every time he mentioned it. Easy as pie.

But the Master Persuader didn't want the critics to be silenced. He wanted them to make border control the biggest issue in the campaign just by talking nonstop about how Trump's "wall" was impractical. As long as people were talking about the wall, Trump was the most important person in the conversation. The Master Persuader moves energy and attention to where it helps him most.

And what about the facts and details? Not so important. Those can get worked out later.

I don't believe Trump purposely injects errors into his work except in the form of over-simplification and hyperbole, as in the wall example. That stuff is intentional for sure. But for the smaller "errors" it is more that he doesn't bother to correct himself. I use a similar technique with my blog when someone points out a typo. Sometimes I leave the typo because it makes you pause and reread the sentence a few times to figure out what the typo was supposed to mean. The "mistake" attracts your energy to my writing, and that's what a writer wants. I want your focus.

PERSUASION TIP 5

An intentional "error" in the details of your message will attract criticism. The attention will make your message rise in importance—at least in people's minds—simply because everyone is talking about it.

Some mistakes are just ordinary mistakes. But when you see a consistent stream of "mistakes" from a Master Persuader, be open to the possibility that some of those mistakes are about controlling your focus and energy.

When you first saw the title of this book, did you think to yourself that Trump doesn't say "bigly," he says "big league"? If you noticed my title "error," it probably helped you remember the book. And now whenever you hear the words "bigly" or "big league" in some other context, it will make you think of this book. The things you think about the most, and remember best, seem more important to you than other things. That's the persuasion I engineered into the title.

During the presidential campaign, it seemed that candidate Trump was making one factual error after another. Social media and the mainstream media were in a feeding frenzy. They called him a liar, a con man, and just plain stupid. Some went so far as to question his sanity.

Even more puzzling, Trump often stuck to his claims after the media thoroughly debunked them in front of the world. He still didn't budge. It was mind-boggling. No one was quite sure if the problem was his honesty, his lack of homework, or some sort of brain problem. But one thing we all knew for sure was that it was hard to ignore.

FACTS ARE WEAKER THAN FICTION

If you have ever tried to talk someone out of their political beliefs by providing facts, you know it doesn't work. That's because people think they have their own facts. Better facts. And if they *know* they don't have better facts, they change the subject. People are not easily switched from one political opinion to another. And facts are weak persuasion.

So Trump ignores facts whenever they are inconvenient. I know you don't want to think this works in terms of persuasion. But it does.

And I know you want to believe that having a president who ignores facts makes the world a worse place, in a number of vague ways that you can't quite articulate. But Trump tends to be directionally accurate on the important stuff, and the little stuff never seems to matter.

I want to be clear that I'm *not expressing a preference for ignoring facts*. I'm simply saying that a Master Persuader can do it and still come out ahead, no matter how many times the media points out the errors.

The average consumer of political news can hold only a handful of issues in his head. Any of the lesser topics get flushed out of memory. So Trump can invent any reality he wants for the less important topics. All you will remember is that he provided his reasons, he didn't apologize, and his opponents called him a liar like they always do.

> **True story:** Ten minutes ago I read a long list of Trump's tweets that *PolitiFact* judged to be factually inaccurate. I can recall only a few of them. They all blended together in my mind, and none made much of an impression. I had no personal or emotional connection to any of them. They were just background noise.[2]

If Trump had *apologized* for any of his factual "errors," I would remember whatever alleged wrongness triggered the apology. That would stick in my mind. I assume that's at least *partly* why he doesn't do apologies. Apologizing would be a sign of weakness and invite continual demands for more apologies. In Trump's specific case, apologies wouldn't have helped his campaign because there would have been too many demands for them. But in the case of normal people who are not Master Persuaders and only occasionally make public mistakes, apologies are still usually the right way to go.

If I haven't yet persuaded you that "mistakes" can be useful in persuasion, consider a small 2012 study by researcher Daniel Oppenheimer that found students had better recall when a font was *harder* to read.[3] Oppenheimer explains the unexpected result by noting that people slow down and concentrate harder to compensate for the hard-to-read font. That extra concentration is what makes lasting memories form.

For more science on the topic of how intentional "mistakes" can aid in memory retention, I recommend the book *Impossible to Ignore*, by Dr. Carmen Simon. The gist of it is that you need to surprise the brain or make it work a little extra to form memories. Our brains automatically delete our routine memories fairly quickly. Most of us don't know what we were doing on this day a year ago. But we easily remember things that violate our expectations.

A good general rule is that people are more influenced by visual persuasion, emotion, repetition, and simplicity than they are by details and facts. Trump inaccurately described his plans for the wall—it probably won't be a physical wall for the entire border span—and that lowered his credibility and tainted his brand. But he makes up for it by using solid-gold visual persuasion, calls to emotion, simplicity, repetition, and the "mistake" itself to make his wall idea compelling. If you're using super strong persuasion, you can be wrong on the facts, and even the logic of your argument, and still win.

I will pause here to tell you that while there is lots of science behind the best ways to influence people, choosing among the many ways to persuade via "surprising the brain" can be more art than science. No two situations are alike, so knowing what methods of persuasion worked in a different context might not help you in your current situation.

Warning: Intentionally ignoring facts and logic in public is a dangerous strategy unless you are a Master Persuader with thick skin and an appetite for risk. Most of us don't have the persuasion skills, risk profile, and moral flexibility to pull it off.

We don't know for sure that Trump came out ahead by oversimplifying his wall idea to the point where it sounded crazy to critics and even some supporters. But in my judgment, he probably did come out ahead. By inauguration day, we were talking about the costs and the details of the wall; the country had already accepted that the wall would probably get built, at least in part. And in the long run, presidents are judged by their success. Love it or hate it, historians will someday probably judge Trump's wall to be a presidential success story. Success cures most types of "mistakes."

PERSUASION VOCABULARY

I created my own vocabulary about persuasion during the election, on top of some vocabulary from the field of cognitive science. I'll explore all of the concepts listed here in more detail later. This alphabetized list is provided as a guide in case you later want to refresh your memory.

Anchor

An anchor is a thought that influences people toward a persuader's preferred outcome. For example, a big opening demand in a negotiation will form a mental anchor that will bias negotiations toward that high offer.

Cognitive Dissonance

Cognitive dissonance is a condition of mind in which evidence conflicts with a person's worldview to such a degree that the person spontaneously generates a hallucination to rationalize the incongruity.

Confirmation Bias

Confirmation bias is the human tendency to irrationally believe new information supports your existing worldview even when it doesn't.

Filter

I use the word "filter" to describe the way people frame their observations of reality. The key idea behind a filter is that it does not necessarily give its user an accurate view of reality. The human brain is not capable of comprehending truth at a deep level.

Godzilla
"Godzilla" was my nickname for one of the most powerful persuaders in the world. You'll find out more about Godzilla later.

The High-Ground Maneuver
The High-Ground Maneuver is a persuasion method that involves elevating a debate from the details on which people disagree to a higher concept on which everyone agrees.

Linguistic Kill Shot
A linguistic kill shot is a nickname or short set of words so persuasive that it can end an argument or create a specific outcome.

Master Persuader
A Master Persuader is one who has such mastery of the tools of persuasion that he or she can change the world. Master Persuaders are rare.

Moist Robot
Moist robot is my framing of human beings as programmable entities. If you provide the right inputs, you get the right outputs.

Mole (the Mole)
In the context of this book, the Mole is an imagined traitorous helper for the Clinton campaign who intentionally made all the wrong choices in terms of persuasion.

Pacing and Leading
Pacing involves matching the person you plan to persuade in as many ways as possible, including the way the person thinks, speaks, breathes, and moves. Pacing builds trust because people see you as being the same

as them. After pacing, a persuader can then lead, and the subject will be comfortable following.

Persuasion Stack
A persuasion stack is a collection of persuasion-related skills that work well together.

Second Dimension
The second dimension describes the most common view of reality—the one in which we believe facts and logic are important to our decisions. This view says humans are reasonable 90 percent of the time, but every now and then we get a bit crazy.

Setting the Table
Setting the table refers to managing an opponent's first impressions before negotiations begin.

Tells
I borrowed this term from poker. In a poker context, it means that a player is giving off a signal—a tell—about how good his cards are. In the context of persuasion, a tell is a signal that someone has been persuaded. But I also use the word generically to indicate any kind of signal.

Thinking Past the Sale
Thinking past the sale is a persuasion technique in which a subject is prompted to imagine what happens after a decision has been made, to bias the person toward making the decision.

Third Act
In movie terms, the Third Act is the point in the story in which the hero's situation looks most dire. I use this terminology to describe any situation in which reality is likely to follow a traditional movie form.

Third Dimension
The third dimension is where trained persuaders operate. This worldview says humans are irrational 90 percent of the time. The only exceptions are when decisions have no emotional content.

Two Movies on One Screen
Two movies on one screen is how I describe the phenomenon in which observers can see the same information and interpret it as supporting two entirely different stories.

Please refer back to this list if you want to refresh your memory of a concept.

PART 2

HOW TO SEE REALITY IN A MORE USEFUL WAY

THE MYTH OF THE
RATIONAL MIND

Students of philosophy remember that Plato talked about the subjective nature of our personal realities in "The Allegory of the Cave" (*Republic*, 514a–520a). Plato asked us to imagine a group of people who lived their lives chained to a wall of a cave that faces another wall. On the wall they face, they see shadows of other people walking around in front of a fire elsewhere in the cave, but there is no way for the prisoners to see the other people directly. To this group of cave prisoners, the shadows themselves appear to be real creatures living independent lives. The prisoners would have no reason to think otherwise because the shadows would act and move like living creatures.

If you released the cave prisoners, they would soon learn about the properties of fire and shadows, and they would have to reinterpret their entire reality to fit the new data. The point of Plato's allegory is that—figuratively speaking—we humans might be chained to a cave created by our own faulty brains and senses, experiencing a shadow world that is entirely different from objective reality.

Other famous philosophers, notably David Hume (born 1711), have questioned the nature of reality in terms of the existence of free will. If, as some philosophers claim, humans have no free will, and we are nothing but victims of cause and effect, that means our common view of reality is absurd. In this model of the world, we are little more than meat robots who wrongly believe we control our own decisions and actions.

Famous German philosopher Immanuel Kant (born 1724) held that the human mind creates the structure of human experience. He explained that our brains don't have direct access to base reality—we have to settle for interpreting the input from our faulty senses. Kant uses a lot of words to say reality isn't necessarily anything like the way we perceive it.

For the purpose of this book, you don't need to accept any of these philosophical interpretations of reality. I only mention them to show that smart people throughout history have made arguments about the subjective nature of reality that are compatible with what you will read in these pages.

In more recent times, cognitive psychologists and physicists have discovered a lot of eye-opening stuff about the limits of human rationality. For example, Dan Ariely, a professor of psychology and behavioral economics at Duke University, has written and lectured extensively on the topic of how humans *believe* they are using facts and reason to make decisions but in reality are easily swayed by bias from lots of different sources. Ariely wrote *Predictably Irrational* (2008).

The most famous voice in this realm is Robert Cialdini, a Regents' Professor Emeritus of psychology and marketing at Arizona State University, and past visiting professor of marketing, business, and psychology at Stanford University. Cialdini's two best-selling books, *Influence* (1984) and *Pre-Suasion* (2016), are master classes in the irrational nature of human decision making.

One place you would expect to find the highest level of human rationality is in financial markets, because trillions of dollars are on the line. But we don't see that rationality, not from common investors and not even from financial professionals. Princeton economist Burton Malkiel taught us about irrational investors in his book *A Random Walk Down Wall Street* (1973). More recently, philosopher and statistician Nassim Nicholas Taleb wrote the hugely influential book *The Black Swan* (2007), which explains our human tendency to consistently misinterpret what we observe.

And what do physicists say about the nature of reality? That's a mixed bag of weirdness. Much of what we know to be true by experiment makes absolutely no sense to our limited human brains. Two of my favorite examples are *quantum entanglement* and the *double-slit experiment*. I'll spare you the wonky science, but if you do some reading on those topics, you will quickly learn that the human brain doesn't have the capacity to understand the nature of reality.

Philosopher Nick Bostrom takes things one step further by asking whether we are a "real" species or a simulation created by an intelligent civilization that came before. This idea comes from the simple fact that we will someday be able to create software simulations that believe they are real creatures. And when we achieve that level of technical proficiency, we're unlikely to stop with one simulation of that type. In the long run, you could expect far more simulated realities than the real one that started it all. So the math of it says we are far more likely to be a simulation than an original species. The interesting thing here is that neither the real species nor the simulations would be in a position to know which one they are. (But just for fun, in appendix C, I propose a way to figure out whether you are real or simulated.)

I mention these brilliant philosophers and scientists because they would all agree there are real limits on both human perception and human rationality.

I encourage you to remain skeptical about any details in this book, but it might help you to know I'm in good company—philosophically speaking—on the big picture: *Humans think they are rational, and they think they understand their reality. But they are wrong on both counts.*

HOW STRONG IS PERSUASION?

Want to see something freaky?

Set this book aside and do an Internet search for "the McGurk effect." Click on the first video you see. It is short. And it will blow your mind when you see how powerful persuasion can be.

Near the start of the clip, you see a close-up of a man's mouth while he repeats, "Bah, bah, bah, bah, bah." You recognize his lips as forming the *B* in "bah," and it all makes sense.

Then things get weird.

The soundtrack stays the same, but the man moves his lips as if he is forming the sound "fa, fa, fa" instead of "bah, bah, bah." And while you watch, as if by magic, your brain turns the sound "bah" into "fa." You know this is an illusion, and you know how they are doing it. And yet it still works. You can go back and forth between the lips that seem to be saying "fa" and the ones that seem to be saying "bah." In reality, the sound is "bah" all the way from start to finish, but your brain will instantly translate the "bah" into "fa" when the lips on the video are moving as if they are creating an *F* sound.

This is a great example of how visual persuasion is more powerful than auditory persuasion. Our visual sense *changes what we are hearing in real time*, even when we know the illusion.

If you don't have time to watch the video right now, make a point of doing it before you finish the book. You won't fully appreciate the power of persuasion until you do.

The main theme of this book is that humans are not rational. We bounce from one illusion to another, all the while thinking we are seeing something we call reality. The truth is that facts and reason don't have much influence on our decisions, except for trivial things, such as putting gas in your car when you are running low. On all the important stuff, we are emotional creatures who make decisions first and rationalize them after the fact.

If you are normal, or anything like normal, you probably think I am exaggerating about how irrational we human beings are. Perhaps you don't *feel* irrational. But consider the U.S. election of 2016, in which Donald J. Trump unexpectedly beat Hillary Clinton in the Electoral College to win the election. I think it is obvious that roughly half of the people in the United States made a deeply irrational decision in that election. But which half?

As a general rule, irrational people don't know they are irrational. After the election results came in, both halves of the country accused the other half of being irrational.

As a trained hypnotist, I can tell you with confidence that both halves were right.

THE PERSUASION FILTER

The common view of reality is that the way *you* see the world is not only accurate but universally shared. For all I know, that might be true. But it might also be the case that reality is something quite different from what you perceive. That possibility might feel unlikely to you. Watch me change your mind. I'll do it by explaining my personal journey through what I call the filters.

The key concept of a filter is that it is *not* intended to give you an accurate view of reality. All it is supposed to do is give you better results than other filters. And I propose that the best way to objectively determine the usefulness of a filter is by asking if it makes you happy and also does a good job of predicting the future. The Persuasion Filter (the main topic of this book) does a great job of making people happy, or so I observe. And it did a great job predicting a number of unlikely events in the presidential election of 2016. That's what I call a good filter.

What I *don't* claim is that the Persuasion Filter is an *accurate* view of reality. I have no reason to believe humans evolved with the capability to understand their reality. That capability was not important to survival. When it comes to evolution, any illusion that keeps us alive long enough to procreate is good enough.

I'll give you a tour of the filters I have used over my lifetime to give you an idea of what I mean.

THE SANTA CLAUS FILTER

When I was a child, it was customary for adults to indoctrinate kids with an entertaining belief in magic of all kinds. For several years of my youth, I thought Santa Claus was real. I also believed in the Tooth Fairy, the Easter Bunny, and Superman.

My filter on life allowed all sorts of magical creatures to exist. The interesting part—and the lesson here—is that this total misconception about reality did an excellent job of keeping me happy and predicting the future. There was no penalty for being totally wrong about reality.

I liked toys, and I liked knowing Santa was efficient, punctual, immortal, and suspiciously generous. I liked knowing that the Tooth Fairy and the Easter Bunny would deliver the goods too. It was a great filter on reality until I was old enough to realize there were simply too many chimneys and too little time for Santa to get the job done. And his sled was totally undersized. The numbers didn't add up. The other magical creatures that inhabited my filter also faded in the light of what I assumed was my higher level of knowledge and reason.

But I was wrong. All I did was move to another filter with new characters.

THE CHURCH FILTER

From the ages of about six to eleven, I attended Sunday school at the Methodist church that was a short walk from my house. I believed everything the church told me because I didn't see any reason they would put so much energy into a centuries-long, elaborate lie. And I assumed all those people couldn't be wrong.

As a child, I understood that other religions existed. But the Methodist Church explained away that discrepancy in my filter by saying all the other religions were wrong. That seemed reasonable to me. And it seemed that 100 percent of the people in my small town of Windham, New York, were Christians of one flavor or another. In hindsight, I assume the atheists were just staying off the radar.

My church filter worked great most of the time. I was happy that I would go to heaven. But the filter didn't seem to do a great job of predicting anything while I was still alive. Prayers didn't seem to influence my outcomes in any reliable way. And no one could predict the next miracle, or the birth of the next saint. I was starting to have my doubts about the church filter.

One day in Sunday school we learned a Bible story about Jonah and the giant fish. The quick version of the story is that Jonah was about to drown in the ocean and God sent a giant fish to save him. The fish accomplished this task by swallowing Jonah whole. Jonah then lived for three days in the belly of the fish, praying to God. After three days, God told the fish to spit out Jonah, and it did. Miraculously (literally), Jonah was none the worse for living in stomach acid without oxygen for three days.

That was the tipping point for me. I called a meeting with my mother and announced that I was discontinuing my religious education. I explained my new hypothesis that she and all other believers were being duped for reasons I couldn't understand, but I planned to get to the bottom of it. My mother listened to my reasoning, acknowledged that I was making a well-informed decision, and never asked me to attend church again. My mom was awesome that way.

Once the church filter fell away, I suddenly found myself living in an absurd world. According to my new worldview, I was the only person— as far as I knew—who could see religion for the scam that it was. Obviously there were plenty of nonbelievers in the world, but they were invisible to me in my pre-Internet, small-town life. I needed a new filter to describe how an eleven-year-old boy could be the only one in the world who saw reality for what it really was. To explain my situation I came up with . . .

THE ALIEN EXPERIMENT FILTER

The alien experiment filter imagined that intelligent creatures from another world impregnated my mother so they could find out what happens when humans and aliens mate. According to that filter, the aliens were watching me at all times. I accepted this as true (enough) for several years of my childhood.

The alien experiment filter did a good job of explaining why I was so different from the people in my town, but it didn't make me happy, and it wasn't any good for predicting what would happen next. It wasn't a useful filter. Eventually I dropped that filter in favor of . . .

THE ATHEIST FILTER

The atheist filter imagines that there is no supreme being. It also imagines that humans are rational creatures and they can understand their environment through observation, science, and reason. This filter was a perfect fit for a rebellious young man. It gave me something juicy to argue about, and I did, whenever anyone would listen. I enjoyed the debates, but I can't say that my atheist filter ever made me happy. Nor did it do a great job of predicting the future, except that I could predict that my prayers would not be answered, and no miracles would happen while I was watching. But those are special cases. As a general rule, I couldn't predict anything using the atheist filter. The atheist filter might turn out to be one of the more accurate views of reality, but that mattered less to me than the fact that it wasn't useful. It didn't make me happy and it didn't help me predict what would happen next. But there were more filters to come.

THE WEED FILTER

I smoked a lot of marijuana in college. One of the most puzzling aspects of being high was that the people around me who were *not* high seemed nicer than usual. For years I assumed I was only *imagining* that people were being extra nice to me when I was high. The simplest explanation for my subjective experience was that the drug was altering my perception of the world.

I started to feel as if I had one reality when I was normal and an entirely different reality when I was high. The interesting thing is that both of those realities worked fine. When I was high, I could still navigate the world and do all the things that people do. There were a few activities, such as studying for tests, that I didn't do as well when high. And driving was a bad idea. But for most daily activities there was no important difference in how I performed. That's when I started to realize that people could be living in different realities while inhabiting the same room. I knew from my own experience that I could experience two realities in the same room just by going from normal to high.

In later years I came to understand why everyone seemed so much nicer to me when I was high. It turns out that people *were* actually nicer to me. And there is a perfectly good reason: My cheery and relaxed attitude while high was rubbing off on the people around me. My other reality—the one in which I was *not* high—brought out my more intense, ambitious, and introspective personality. People respond to that personality with less friendliness because I look like I'm all business, and it rubs off on them. I wasn't *perceiving* reality to be different when I was high—I was *causing* it to be different.

Here again we can see that the true nature of reality—if such a thing exists—was somewhat irrelevant to my day-to-day life. My reality made perfect sense when I believed I was only imagining that people were acting nicer to me when I was high. And reality still made sense when I realized (or believed) I was causing that niceness by my own demeanor. The choice of filter didn't make much difference to my life.

The weed filter was a big improvement over my past filters because it made me happy (obviously), but it also had some predictive power. When I was high, I knew people would respond to me in a certain way, on average, and they did. Or so it seemed. And that's all that mattered. But the weed filter is limited, at best.

THE MUSHROOM FILTER

I moved to San Francisco at age twenty-one, and a friend talked me into trying psychedelic mushrooms. It was the best day of my life, at least in terms of pure joy. And that isn't an exaggeration. No other experience has ever come close. But while the pleasure was temporary—literally just a spike in certain brain chemistry—the experience left me permanently changed. As those of you who have tried psychedelics already know, words can't describe the experience. But I'll try to explain it in the limited context of filters.

When you are on mushrooms, you understand the world around you, and you can operate within it. But at the same time, you become aware that your interpretation of your reality is fluid. You see ordinary items almost as if you are an alien visiting this strange world for the first time, but for some odd reason you know what everything is and what it does. In other words, you become aware that your perceptions are independent from the underlying reality. That awareness never leaves you. Once you understand your experience of life as an *interpretation* of reality, you can't go back to your old way of thinking. After taking psychedelics, you might stop seeing your old interpretation of reality as the only "true" version. That's what happened to me.

Kids, please don't take drugs. Drugs can be dangerous. I don't recommend trying marijuana or psychedelics. You'll get a similar perceptual shift by reading this book. I designed it to do exactly that. In other words, I took all of those drugs so you don't have to. You're welcome.

THE MOIST ROBOT FILTER

My current filter on life is what I call the moist robot filter. I wrote about it in detail in my book *How to Fail at Almost Everything and Still Win Big*. The summary is that human brains are moist computers that can be reprogrammed if you know where the user interface is. For example, we know that going to school can change the physical structure of your brain by making it form new connections and new memories. That part is obvious. But there are lots of other ways to reprogram your brain to develop useful habits, change your energy level, hack your happiness, and more. The moist robot filter assumes your brain is subject to the laws of physics and doesn't have any magical qualities such as free will or a soul.

For our purposes here, we don't need to debate whether humans have free will or souls. Remember, filters are *not about knowing reality*. The role of a filter is limited to making you happy and helping you predict the future. Humans don't always need to know the true nature of reality in order to live well. The moist robot filter is the filter that makes me happiest, and it does the best job of predicting. The Persuasion Filter—the topic of this book—is a subset of the moist robot worldview. As moist robots, we are easily influenced by emotional and irrational factors. If you learn the mechanisms of this influence, you have found the user interface for human beings. So when I talk about the Persuasion Filter, you should understand that it is fully compatible with the moist robot idea. Or to put it another way, my *How to Fail* book was about persuading yourself, and this book is about persuading others.

THE PERSUASION FILTER

The most common opinion that we humans have of ourselves is that we are rational creatures—let's say 90 percent of the time, anyway. But every now and then we get a little emotional and temporarily lose our sense of

reason. That's how most people see the world. I did too until I trained to become a hypnotist.

Hypnotists see the world differently. From our perspective, people are irrational 90 percent of the time but don't know it. We can be rational in trivial situations—such as deciding what time to leave the house to drive to work. But we are almost never rational when it comes to matters of love, family, pets, politics, ego, entertainment, and almost anything else that matters to us emotionally. When our feelings turn on, our sense of reason shuts off. The freaky part is that we don't recognize when it is happening to us. We think we are reasonable and rational most of the time. But what hypnotists have long known, and scientists have in recent years confirmed, is that our decisions are often made without appeal to the rational parts of our brains. We literally make our decisions first and then create elaborate rationalizations for them after the fact.

Freaky, right?

The grand illusion of life is that our minds have the capacity to understand reality. But human minds didn't evolve to understand reality. We didn't need that capability. A clear view of reality wasn't necessary for our survival. Evolution cares only that you survive long enough to procreate. And that's a low bar. The result is that each of us is, in effect, living in our own little movie that our brain has cooked up for us to explain our experiences.

Let me give you an example.

Let's say that you believe you are reincarnated from an earlier life in which you were a Tibetan monk. And let's say I think my prophet flew to heaven on a winged horse. Those are very different movies. But it doesn't matter to our survival that we are experiencing different realities. As long as humans procreate and create more humans, evolution has done its job. Evolution doesn't care if you see the world for what it is. It only cares that you make more of yourself.

Here's an example of why the idea that humans are rational is pure nonsense. One of my Twitter followers copied President Trump's inauguration speech and showed it to a "leftist friend," telling him it was President Obama's speech. His friend loved it.

I watched President Trump's inauguration address on television while live-streaming to several hundred people on the Periscope app. Most of the people who commented to me directly were touched by the inclusiveness and optimism in Trump's message. There were many tears.

But within the hour, I received an e-mail from one of my best friends, a virulent anti-Trumper, who said this:

> I was quite surprised by Trump's speech. I thought all inaugural addresses include soaring language and hope for the future. This one sounded like his stump speech (but without the insults). Lots of anti-Washington rhetoric. It was the most negative tone I can remember hearing. No "Ask not what your country can do for you." No "shining city on the hill."
>
> I also expected to hear more reaching out to others. "Not all of you voted for me, but I will be the President of all the people." That used to be pretty standard stuff as well. I guess Trump just does it his way, and we need to get used to it.

That interpretation is literally the opposite of what I heard and saw. This odd difference in observation is not unusual. Both my friend and I follow politics. We're both smart. (He's smarter.) Neither of us lied about our reaction to Trump's speech. But we saw entirely different movies playing on the same screen at the same time. If you think this different-movies situation is rare, you're living in what I call the second dimension. In the third dimension, where persuasion rules, it is entirely normal and routine for different movies to play on the same screen at the same time.

But if each of us is living in our own little movie, which one is best?

I submit that the best filter on politics is the one that makes you happy and is the most accurate at predicting what will happen next. I used the Persuasion Filter to predict Trump's presidency when others thought it was madness. And I predicted a lot of steps along the way that I'll describe in this book. All of my predictions were public. You can check them for yourself.

But even if I were to convince you that the Persuasion Filter is the best way to predict the future, you will still wonder how humans could be so delusional and not realize it. And to understand that you must understand two concepts: cognitive dissonance and confirmation bias. These two concepts explain almost everything that puzzles you about why people act the way they do. And they explain the 2016 election in a way nothing else can.

COGNITIVE DISSONANCE

Wikipedia gives us a useful definition of cognitive dissonance:

In psychology, cognitive dissonance is the mental stress or discomfort experienced by an individual who holds two or more contradictory beliefs, ideas, or values at the same time; performs an action that is contradictory to their beliefs, ideas, or values; or is confronted by new information that conflicts with existing beliefs, ideas, or values.[1]

The science around cognitive dissonance is deep, but you don't need any of that depth to be a good persuader. All you need to understand is the basic idea of cognitive dissonance and—this is important—*how often it happens in your daily experience.* I told you the normal view of the world is that we are rational 90 percent of the time and we get a little crazy 10 percent of the time. The Persuasion Filter's view of the world is that we're *irrational* 90 percent of the time. And one of the biggest sources of this irrationality is cognitive dissonance.

The most common trigger for cognitive dissonance is when a person's self-image doesn't fit their observations. For example, if you believe you are a smart and well-informed person, and then you do something that is clearly dumb, it sends you into a state of cognitive dissonance. And once you are in that uncomfortable state of mind, your brain automatically generates an illusion to solve the discomfort. In this situation, your brain would tell you the new information was inaccurate. The alternative is to believe that you are dumb, and that violates your self-image. You don't like to change your self-image unless it is in the direction of improvement.

Our egos prevent us from imagining we are irrational 90 percent of the time. When we recognize ourselves acting irrationally, the simplest course of action for the brain is to generate an illusion that explains it all away. And so it does. Automatically. The fun part is that we are not aware when it is happening. Others might be able to see it happening in you as clear as day. But by its nature, cognitive dissonance is invisible to the person experiencing it.

HOW TO SPOT COGNITIVE DISSONANCE

When you experience cognitive dissonance, you spontaneously generate a hallucination that becomes your new reality. To outside observers, the hallucination might look ridiculous. But to the person experiencing the hallucination it all makes perfect sense. So the first thing you need to know about cognitive dissonance is that you can often recognize it in others, and they can recognize it in you, but recognizing it in yourself is rare.

Trained hypnotists can sometimes recognize cognitive dissonance when they are in it. Cognitive scientists can probably do it sometimes too. But for those untrained in the art of persuasion, experiencing cognitive dissonance feels exactly like an accurate view of reality. You can't tell the difference.

The first "tell" for cognitive dissonance is the absurdity of the rationalization. For example, you might be friends with a cigarette smoker who claims smoking won't hurt him because he knows someone who smoked a pack a day and lived to be a hundred years old. The person who makes that sort of argument is simply addicted to smoking but doesn't like to think of himself as being unwise or unable to quit. That would violate the person's self-image. To keep his self-image intact, the smoker generates a personal illusion in which he is one of the few people in the world who are immune to lung cancer and somehow know it.

We live in an irrational world in which people are continually saying and doing absurd-looking things. Sometimes those people are just dumb, and that's the entire explanation for why they are doing dumb-looking things. Sometimes the problem is on your end, and the things that others are doing look absurd to you only because you don't understand why they do what they do. There can be lots of false positives when you look for cognitive dissonance because there is so much run-of-the-mill irrationality everywhere that any special flavor of it can easily hide. The best way to know you are seeing cognitive dissonance and not routine irrationality is to look for the trigger. The trigger is whatever made the person realize that their own actions were in conflict with their self-image.

In the smoking example, some people admit they are addicted and say they enjoy smoking, and so they put up with the high risks. Those people are probably *not* experiencing cognitive dissonance because they understand the risks and causation correctly.

But a smoker who refuses to admit that addiction is central to the habit—perhaps because the person has too much confidence in his own self-control—has to invent a hallucination for why a smart person with self-control would do such a damaging thing as smoking. That incongruity is the trigger. The person's self-image doesn't match his own actions.

The presidential election of 2016 provided the biggest trigger for cognitive dissonance you might ever see in your lifetime. It had all the elements for generating mass hallucinations. From the moment that Trump announced his candidacy, the professional political class started mocking his intelligence, his commitment, his talent, and—most important—his chances of winning. The pundits believe they are smart, and they believe they can see the world for what it is. And in the case of Trump, it seemed to them the easiest prediction in the world, at least for people so well informed and rational. What mattered the most here, in terms of the trigger, is not that these folks were so wrong. People are wrong all the time, and it doesn't always cause hallucinations. The key variable in this case was their *certainty*. And it was *public* certainty, repeated loudly and often. Their opinions of Trump became part of their self-image. They saw themselves as the smart ones, in stark contrast to what they imagined were the Trump supporters with their mullets and pickup trucks.

And then Trump won. By a comfortable margin, at least in the Electoral College, which is the only place it matters. Trump lost the popular vote, but that was a case of losing a game he wasn't playing.

Trump's win was the trigger. The pundits and the voters who believed they were the smart ones suddenly learned they were not. And they learned it in the clearest possible way. They were wrong about the voters in swing states. They were wrong to trust the polls. They were wrong to underestimate Trump's intelligence. They were wrong to underestimate his campaign's effectiveness. They were wrong about his need to do traditional advertising. They were wrong about his ground game. They were wrong in thinking that his provocative statements would end him. They were wrong to believe that his alleged scandals would end him. They were wrong about his tweeting being a bad idea. They were wrong that Trump would cause down-ticket Republicans to lose. They were wrong about just about everything.

They were so wrong that Republicans came to occupy the White House, control Congress, and eventually control the Supreme Court. That is wrongness on a scale you rarely see.

To make matters worse, they had to watch a number of smart people such as Ann Coulter, Mike Cernovich, Stefan Molyneux, and Milo Yiannopoulos call this entire process correctly from start to finish. If everyone in the world had been wrong about Trump, it would be easier to write it off as a fluke that no reasonable person could have seen coming. That wasn't an option in this case because a number of smart and prominent Trump supporters *were* right about everything, from the start. We gave our reasons—loudly and often—and showed our work all the way.

A *year before the election* I said this in my blog:

Trump's persuasion skills would set off a swarm of competing (and wrong) explanations for why Trump is defying expectations.

In other words, I saw the conditions forming for massive cognitive dissonance long before anyone else mentioned it publicly, as far as I know. That's how a background in persuasion lets you see the future that others can't. It's a learned skill, not a psychic power. If you know what causes cognitive dissonance, you can sometimes see the conditions forming from miles away.

And sure enough, Trump's win set off a cluster bomb of cognitive dissonance the likes of which history rarely sees. To untrained observers—voters and pundits alike—the public reaction looked like a combination of anger, disappointment, fear, and shock. But to trained persuaders, it was a front-row seat to a show of cognitive dissonance so pure and so deep that it was, frankly, beautiful.

Most people didn't appreciate the show. What they saw instead was an endless stream of after-the-fact "reasons" to explain their new reality in which someone like Trump could get elected.

A few days after the election, CNN.com listed twenty-four different theories from pundits to explain why Trump won. I present them below as entries that don't make complete sense out of context, but trust me when I say the context doesn't matter in this specific case. Many of the explanations sound quite reasonable, but the credibility of the explanations is not related to my point about spotting cognitive dissonance. The tell is *not the quality* of the explanations. The tell is *how many* of them there are.

If you have a situation that can be explained with one reasonable explanation, that reason might be close to reality. But having *lots of different* explanations is usually a clear tell for cognitive dissonance. Having multiple explanations—no matter how reasonable they sound after the fact—means people are trying to make sense of their observations, and they are generating different illusions to do it. Here are some of the explanations for Trump's unexpected win, from CNN's article.

1. Facebook was unable or unwilling to crack down on fake news.
2. Social media.
3. Low voter turnout.
4. Celebrity outlasts substance.

5. White women were more important than anyone thought.

6. White male resentment.

7. Russian hacking and fake news.

8. The Left and coastal elites shamed Trump supporters.

9. Rural midwesterners don't get out of the house enough.

10. The Democratic Party establishment didn't push Bernie Sanders.

11. Reagan Democrats surged in Michigan and the Midwest.

12. The media focused too much on millennial voters, not enough on older white males.

13. Gary Johnson and Jill Stein took votes.

14. College-educated Americans are out of touch.

15. Political correctness set off a nasty backlash.

16. Trump listened to the American people.

17. Americans are biased against the ruling class in Washington DC.

18. Voters believed the system was corrupt.

19. Trump remembered "forgotten men, women" of America.

20. Democrats focused more on turning out supporters than on growing the base.

21. The Democratic National Committee selected the less competitive candidate.

22. Not because of racism. Voters just preferred Trump.

23. FBI Director Comey's announcements about Clinton's e-mails came just weeks before election day.

24. Clinton was a bad candidate.

The media explainers weren't done yet. Some experts pointed out that the candidate of change has a big advantage, so we should have seen it coming. But if the "change" pattern is so predictive, why didn't the experts use it to predict? And why do we believe that all the other Republican candidates would have lost to Clinton when, after all, they too represented big change?

And nowhere in the list of explanations for Trump's win do pundits and pollsters blame themselves for telling Clinton supporters her win was assured. I have to think the media's confidence in her win caused some people to skip voting.

PERSUASION TIP 7

It is easy to fit completely different explanations to the observed facts. Don't trust any interpretation of reality that isn't able to *predict*.

Many of the after-the-fact explanations make perfect sense. But keep in mind that it is easy to fit a wide variety of explanations to the *past*. Trial lawyers do it every day. The prosecution and the defense present two different narratives to explain the observed facts, and both can sound convincing. The prosecution says the accused owned the murder weapon, so obviously he is guilty. The defense points out that the accused had roommates, and they had access to the gun too, so maybe one of the roommates did it. Same facts, different stories. And both stories can sound perfectly credible.

THE AFTER-ELECTION DANGER

After the election results came in, people expected me to gloat. You could say I earned it. I had just pulled off the upset prediction of the century while enduring more than a year of nonstop abuse from pro-Clinton and Republican establishment types. If anyone ever had a good reason to gloat, I did.

But I couldn't. I knew how dangerous the situation was. I knew people would experience a form of temporary insanity. Cognitive dissonance by itself isn't always dangerous. But if you combine that with the illusion that some sort of Hitler had just become leader of the country—and that's what the anti-Trumpers believed—we had a risk of riots, violence, and a breakdown of our entire system.

I wanted to gloat, but I'm a patriot first, and the country needed some calm voices. I took to my blog, Twitter, and Periscope to persuade Trump supporters to back away from the gloating that they too had earned. By this point in the election saga, Trump supporters recognized me as a credible voice about politics. My reputation was reinforced by Trump's win. Suddenly I had influence like never before. I had the ears and eyes of the media. I had a huge audience. And I had a very big problem to help solve.

I don't normally turn up my persuasion powers to weapons grade. But I can. This time, with the republic in the balance, I felt I needed to. And so I picked one of the strongest persuasion tools: the High-Ground Maneuver (described more fully in its own chapter later in the book).

I used my social media platform to remind Trump supporters that they are patriots first, and their country needed them for the healing. I asked them to take punches from Clinton supporters and not fight back. I asked them to avoid gloating in public. I asked them to be the better people. I asked them to earn the leader they believed they elected. In other words, I took them to the high ground.

Did my persuasion make any difference?

There is no way to tell. But I was impressed at how well Trump supporters handled their win. For the most part, they didn't confront protesters. They didn't gloat nearly as much as I would have expected. They found the high ground, perhaps on their own, and simply enjoyed the show as the mainstream media tried to do brain surgery on itself to find out where the problem was.

By election day I had over 100,000 social media followers, and they tweeted and retweeted anything interesting I said. For a year I had been one of them, gaining their trust. When I was ready to lead, they were primed to follow. All the elements were in place for my persuasion to make a huge dent in the national consciousness, both directly and through my influence on other writers. Good ideas travel from person to person, and often they lose their connection to the source over time. It is nearly impossible to measure one person's persuasion in this sort of situation. All I know for sure is that I did my best. That's what my patriotism required. I'm glad it worked out. As I write this, the "Trump is Hitler" illusion has largely passed.

Nice job, Americans, and a hat tip to the founders, who created this robust system. I continue to be astonished at our Constitution's power over our minds. But I shouldn't be surprised, given that Master Persuaders wrote it.

How do I know the founders of America were Master Persuaders?

You'll find out before the end of this book.

SPOTTING TELLS FOR COGNITIVE DISSONANCE

Over the years, I have noticed a variety of tells for when a person is experiencing cognitive dissonance. This comic gives you a classic example of what it looks like.

The comic is based on common patterns I observe on Twitter. When I see someone get triggered into cognitive dissonance—either by me or by anyone else—I often see a similar pattern of response. The pattern is so persistent that it is spooky. And once I describe it, you'll start seeing it all the time.

As far as I can tell, the most frequent tells for cognitive dissonance on Twitter take this form:

[A mocking word or acronym] + [an absurd absolute]

or . . .

[A mocking word or acronym] + [a personal insult that is more aggressive than the situation seems to warrant]

Regarding the first tell, when people do not have rational reasons for their views—and you help them achieve that realization—they typically

and immediately hallucinate that your argument is some kind of absurd absolute instead of whatever reasonable thing you actually said. That instant hallucination provides the critic something with which they can easily disagree. For example, if you make a solid argument on Twitter in favor of private gun ownership, and it triggers cognitive dissonance in some random stranger, you might see a response like this from the stranger: "LOL. I guess you want to give guns to toddlers!"

In that example, the "LOL" is the mocking acronym, and the absurd absolute is the mischaracterization of your opinion as wanting to give guns to toddlers. The most common mocking words and abbreviations on Twitter are these:

- Wow
- OMG
- So . . .
- In other words . . .
- HAHAHAHA! (the exaggerated laugh)
- Dude

The list is not exhaustive, but I think you get the pattern. The start of the tweet generally contains contempt, mocking, or sarcasm. The second part of the tweet includes either an insult that seems too angry for the situation or a mischaracterization of your point as an absurd absolute.

As a public service, I described in my blog a way to know you won an argument on the Internet by spotting cognitive dissonance. Here are some additional tells you might find familiar.

How to Know You Won a Political Debate on the Internet

Posted May 15, 2017

Analogy

Analogies are good for explaining concepts for the first time. But they have no value in debate. Analogies are not logic, and they are not relevant facts. An analogy is literally just two things that remind you of each other on at least one dimension. When I see a cauliflower, it reminds me of a human brain, but that doesn't mean you should eat brains in your salad. When your debate opponents retreat to analogies, it is because they have no rational arguments. You won.

There's a reason your plumber never describes the source of your leak with an analogy. He just points to the problem and says it needs to be repaired or replaced. No one needs an analogy when facts and reason can do the job.

An Attack on the Messenger

When people realize their arguments are not rational, they attack the messenger on the other side. If you have been well behaved in a debate, and you trigger an oversized personal attack, it means you won. When people have facts and reasons in their armory, they use them first. When they run out of rational arguments, they attack the messenger. That is the equivalent of throwing the gun at the monster after you run out of bullets.

People are mean on the Internet all the time. Being an ordinary jerk might not be a tell for cognitive dissonance. But when you see an attack that seems *far angrier than the situation calls for*, that's usually cognitive dissonance.

The Psychic Psychiatrist Illusion

The psychic psychiatrist illusion involves imagining you can discern the inner thoughts and motives of strangers. I'm talking about the *unspoken* thoughts and feelings of strangers, not the things they have actually said. If your debate opponents retreat to magical thinking about their abilities to detect secret motives and mental problems in strangers from a distance, you won.

I'm not aware of any science to back up my description of the tells for cognitive dissonance. But generally speaking, if your debate partner leaves the realm of fact and reason for any of the diversions I mentioned, you just won the debate. Declare victory and bow out.

You can sometimes spot your own cognitive dissonance via the same set of tells you would observe in others. But that is harder because the nature of cognitive dissonance is that the person experiencing it can't see it for what it is. If you catch yourself rationalizing away one of the tells I mentioned in this chapter as not applicable in your situation, that's a red flag you shouldn't ignore. And by the end of this book, you should have a lower confidence in your ability to identify base reality, which gives you psychological permission to be wrong without needing to hallucinate that you are right.

My disclaimer for this lesson: This is my opinion alone, based on observation. I advise you to maintain some skepticism, but watch how often you start seeing the pattern now that I've explained it.

And if you do see the pattern, don't rule out the possibility that you and I are both experiencing confirmation bias and there is no real pattern at all.

CONFIRMATION BIAS

The world can be a confusing place if you don't know what confirmation bias is and how often it occurs in our daily lives. Confirmation bias is the human reflex to interpret any new information as being supportive of the opinions we already hold. And it doesn't matter how poorly the new information fits our existing views. We will twist our minds into pretzels to make the new information feel as if it is consistent with what we "know" to be true.

For example, as I write this chapter, news services are reporting a variety of stories about alleged collusion between Russia and the Trump campaign staff, but we have seen no actual evidence of it. On top of the collusion allegations are stories about alleged Russian "influence" on the election that doesn't involve any collusion; those stories appear to have more substance. But the interesting thing is that the anti-Trumpers and the Trump supporters are seeing different realities based on the same set of reported facts. Trump's enemies say there is so much smoke (Russia-related allegations) that there must be a fire (collusion). Trump's supporters say no evidence has been presented for collusion (true at this writing) and so he has been "proven" innocent of collusion by lack of evidence.

Both positions are nonsense.

The "smoke" that Trump's critics are seeing is largely of their own making. If there are enough Russia-related election stories, and you hear enough people speculate about what *might* have happened, it starts to feel like a mountain of "evidence." Yet no evidence of collusion has been made public (at this writing).

Trump's supporters are just as delusional. They see a lack of evidence as proof of innocence. But you can't prove something doesn't exist just because you didn't see it in the places you looked.

The important takeaway here is that citizens for and against President Trump are looking at the same information and coming to opposite conclusions. And neither of the conclusions is sensible. That's confirmation bias. Obviously every individual is different, but on average, Trump's opponents believe they see something that doesn't exist (evidence of collusion) while Trump's supporters believe they see something else that doesn't exist (proof there was no collusion).

If you don't understand confirmation bias, you might think new information can change people's opinions. As a trained persuader, I know that isn't the case, at least when emotions are involved. People don't change opinions about emotional topics just because some information proved their opinion to be nonsense. Humans aren't wired that way.

Confirmation bias is one of the many reasons you should not solely rely on past experience to predict the future. Those facts that you *think* you know from the past might be confirmation bias, and not facts at all.

Most people know what confirmation bias is, if not by its name, then certainly by personal experience. We all know how hard it is to change a person's mind about anything important, even when all of the facts are on our side. But what nonpersuaders usually don't realize is how prevalent confirmation bias is. Confirmation bias isn't an occasional bug in our human operating system. It *is* the operating system. We are designed by evolution to see new information as supporting our existing opinions, so long as it doesn't stop us from procreating. Evolution doesn't care if you understand your reality. It only cares that you reproduce. It also wants you to conserve energy for the important stuff, such as surviving. The worst thing your brain could do is reinterpret your reality into a whole new movie with each new bit of information. That would be exhausting and without benefit. Instead, your brain takes the path of least resistance and instantly interprets your observations to fit your existing worldview. It's just easier.

MASS DELUSIONS

If you don't know how frequently mass delusions occur in your daily experience, many of your opinions about the world are likely to be nonsense. That's because mass delusions are the norm for humanity, not the exception.

Don't believe me?

It is easy to check. Just ask your neighbors about their religious and political views. You'll find plenty of disagreement with your worldview. And so, according to you, your neighbors and all the people who agree with them must be living in some sort of hallucination. How can they believe they are reincarnated when you know that death means either heaven or hell? You and your neighbor can't both be right. One of you (at least) is experiencing a little piece of a larger mass delusion.

And the problem isn't limited to your neighbors. Millions of people share the same mass delusions (according to you).

Do you remember when millions of Americans believed President Obama was a secret Muslim? That was a mass delusion.

Do you remember when President Trump got elected and there were protests in the street because they thought he was the next Hitler? That was a mass delusion.

Do you remember the dot-com bubble? That was based on mass delusions about the value of money-losing start-ups. Every other financial bubble was also a mass delusion.

Below is a starter list of the more notable mass delusions. *Wikipedia* lists over thirty examples of mass hysteria through the years. But those are only the famous cases. Mass delusions are influencing every one of us all the time. Until the spell is broken, you can't tell you are in one. The examples that follow should be enough for you to see the pattern. Once you see how easily mass delusions start, and how confirmation bias can keep them fueled, you might start to recognize how often it is happening to you in your daily experience.

SALEM WITCH TRIALS

Between 1692 and 1693, authorities executed twenty people in Salem, Massachusetts, for being witches. This is perhaps the most famous case of mass hysteria in American history. It all started when four adolescent girls started having fits that didn't have an obvious cause.[1] In this sort of situation, all it takes is one idiot to suggest witchcraft as the problem, and from that point on, confirmation bias does the rest. Once your brain filter is set to look for witches, all evidence fits into the "witch" frame.

ORSON WELLES'S "THE WAR OF THE WORLDS"

In 1938 author Orson Welles broadcast a radio adaptation of H. G. Wells's book *The War of the Worlds*. People who missed the introduction and tuned in late believed they were hearing a news report of an actual alien invasion of Earth.[2]

This is a rare case of a double mass delusion. The first mass delusion involved listeners misinterpreting the radio program as a news report and believing space aliens were attacking. But that "mass" delusion didn't influence many people because the radio show had a small audience. The *second* mass delusion is that this story was exaggerated in the telling until the public believed it *had* been a mass delusion of national scale. I can confirm that when I was a child, I learned from my parents that the radio program fooled much of the country at the same time. That didn't happen. The program had a small listener base, and anyone who heard the introduction knew it was presented as fiction.

MCMARTIN PRESCHOOL TRIAL

In the 1980s, the operators of a preschool in Manhattan Beach, California, were arrested on charges of abusing 360 kids. The accused were found not guilty on all charges. Later we learned that investigators used an extremely suggestive form of questioning when interviewing the children. The kids made up all sorts of stories in response to how the questions were phrased. None of the stories were true.[3]

I learned in hypnosis class that kids are more suggestible than adults. Anyone with my kind of training would have seen this situation for what it was. By the end of this book, you'll be able to do the same.

TULIP MANIA

In 1637 the Dutch became so enamored with tulips, a flower that was new to them, that they bid up the price of tulip bulbs (the part you plant) to about ten times the annual income of a skilled worker.[4] Everyone understood that the plants were not intrinsically valuable. But as long as people believed the next sucker would buy a bulb for more than the last sucker paid, the price continued to climb. Like all financial bubbles, eventually it popped.

On top of our mass delusions, we also have junk science that is too often masquerading as the real thing. To the extent that people can't tell the difference, that too is a source of mass delusion.

In the 2-D view of the world, mass delusions are rare and newsworthy. But to trained persuaders in the third dimension, mass delusions are the norm. They are everywhere, and they influence every person. This difference in training and experience can explain why people disagree on some of the big issues of the day.

For example, consider the case of global warming. People from the 2-D world assume mass delusions are rare, and they apply that assumption to every topic. So when they notice that most scientists are on the same side, that observation is persuasive to them. A reasonable person wants to be on the same side with the smartest people who understand the topic. That makes sense, right?

But people who live in the 3-D world, where persuasion rules, can often have a different view of climate change because we see mass delusions (even among experts) as normal and routine. My starting bias for this topic is that the scientists could easily be wrong about the horrors of climate change, even in the context of repeated experiments and peer review. Whenever you see a situation with complicated prediction models, you also have lots of room for bias to masquerade as reason. Just tweak the assumptions and you can get any outcome you want.

Now add to that situation the fact that scientists who oppose the climate change consensus have a high degree of career and reputation risk. That's the perfect setup for a mass delusion. You only need these two conditions:

1. Complicated prediction models with lots of assumptions
2. Financial and psychological pressure to agree with the consensus

In the 2-D world, the scientific method and peer review squeeze out the bias over time. But in the 3-D world, the scientific method can't detect bias when nearly everyone including the peer reviewers shares the same mass delusion.

I'm not a scientist, and I have no way to validate the accuracy of the climate model predictions. But if the majority of experts on this topic turn out to be having a mass hallucination, I would consider that an ordinary situation. In my reality, this would be routine, if not expected, whenever there are complicated prediction models involved. That's because I see the world as bristling with mass delusions. I don't see mass delusions as rare.

When nonscientists take sides with climate scientists, they often think they are being supportive of science. The reality is that the nonscientists are not involved in science, or anything like it. They are *taking the word* of scientists. In the 2-D world, that makes perfect sense, because it seems as if thousands of experts can't be wrong. But in the 3-D world, I accept that the experts *could* be right, and perhaps they are, but it would be normal and natural in my experience if the vast majority of climate scientists were experiencing a shared hallucination.

To be clear, I am not saying the majority of scientists are wrong about climate science. I'm making the narrow point that it would be normal and natural for that group of people to be experiencing a mass hallucination that is consistent with their financial and psychological incentives. The scientific method and the peer-review process wouldn't *necessarily* catch a mass delusion during any specific window of time. With science, you never know if you are halfway to the truth or already there. Sometimes it looks the same.

Climate science is a polarizing topic (ironically). So let me just generalize the point to say that compared with the average citizen, trained persuaders are less impressed by experts.

To put it another way, if an ordinary idiot doubts a scientific truth, the most likely explanation for that situation is that the idiot is wrong. But if a trained persuader calls BS on a scientific truth, pay attention.

Do you remember when citizen Trump once tweeted that climate change was a hoax for the benefit of China? It sounded crazy to most of the world. Then we learned that the centerpiece of politics around climate change—the Paris climate accord—was hugely expensive for the United States and almost entirely useless for lowering temperatures. (Experts agree on both points now.) The accord was a good deal for China, in the sense that it would impede its biggest business rival, the United States, while costing China nothing for years. You could say Trump was wrong to call climate change a hoax. But in the context of Trump's normal hyperbole, it wasn't as wrong as the public's mass delusion believed it to be at the time.

I'll concede that citizen Trump did not understand the science of climate change. That's true of most of us. But he still detected a fraud from a distance.

It wasn't luck.

WHEN REALITY BIFURCATED

When the presidential election of 2016 was over, reality split into two movies. Trump supporters believed that they had elected a competent populist to "drain the swamp" and make America great again. Their preferred media sources agreed. But anti-Trumpers had been force-fed, by both the mainstream media and Clinton's campaign, a fire hose of persuasion that said Trump was the next Hitler. In effect, the Trump supporters and the anti-Trumpers woke up in different movies. One movie is a disaster movie and the other is an inspirational story.

The fascinating thing about this situation is each of us can operate in the world and do the things we need to do to survive. You and I can both go shopping, both drive cars, both have jobs and friends. Living in completely different realities is our normal way of living. We usually don't see it so starkly as we did the week after the election.

The two-movie split in our reality wouldn't have happened if Clinton had won, as most experts expected. In that scenario, everyone would simply be living in a world that was a lot like the one they were already in. But Trump's unexpected win created a persuasion bomb that no one knew how to defuse. The anti-Trumpers were locked into their Hitler movie, and confirmation bias would keep them there. It was a terrible situation for a country. And it was an enormous challenge for Trump, the Master Persuader.

It turns out Trump was up to the challenge. The solution to the Hitler

68 WIN BIGLY

PERSUASION TIP 8

People are more influenced by the direction of things than the current state of things.

movie is to act non-Hitlerish in public until people can no longer maintain the Hitler illusion and it falls apart. And that's how Trump and his running mate Pence played it. They quickly moderated some of their more extreme campaign positions so they looked like they were heading *away* from Hitler mode, not toward it. People are more influenced by the *direction* of things than the current state. So Trump changed the direction.

Trump signaled his direction away from authoritarian rule in several high-profile ways.

- President Trump's most notable change involved scaling back his deportation plans by focusing on undocumented immigrants who committed serious crimes *after* entering the country.
- Trump also worked with Congress and the judicial system (like an ordinary politician) trying to get an immigration ban on several countries believed to be high risk in terms of future terrorist attacks. By failing on his initial attempts, and working within the system, he looked nothing like a "strongman" leader.
- Trump dropped support for waterboarding, and he stopped talking about going after the families of terrorists.
- Trump ordered a fifty-nine-Tomahawk-missile attack on a Syrian air base as a response to allegations that Syria used chemical weapons. Even Trump's critics called it measured and "presidential."

Trump's critics strained to maintain their framing of the president as a dictator, but his actions no longer provided the high-quality ammunition that his preelection provocations did. And that allowed the Trump-is-Hitler illusion to begin the process of evaporating. By the time you read this book, some of the events I mentioned might look different. But you can see that Trump got the *direction* right. He was clearly trending away from the Hitler label and toward something that looks more like a regular president.

Trump couldn't fully erase the Hitler illusion until he had another "movie" to replace it in people's heads. Trump created the replacement movie (in part) by using a common business persuasion strategy that I call the new-CEO move. Here's how I described it in my blog after President-elect Trump and VP-elect Pence claimed credit for keeping Ford and Carrier jobs in this country.

Posted December 1, 2016

So what does a Master Persuader do when he needs to create a good first impression to last for years? He looks around for any opportunity that is visible, memorable, newsworthy, true to his brand, and easy to change.

Enter Ford.

Enter Carrier.

Trump and Pence recognized these openings and took them. Political writers will interpret this situation as routine credit grabbing and exaggerated claims. But business writers will recognize Trump's strategy as what I will call the new-CEO move. Smart CEOs try to create visible victories within days of taking the job, to set the tone. It's all about the psychology.

If you are looking at Trump's claims of success with Ford and Carrier in terms of technical accuracy and impact on the economy, you will be underwhelmed. But if you view it through a business filter and understand that psychology is the point of the exercise, you're seeing one of the best new-CEO moves you will ever see.

I'll say this again because it's important. We're all watching closely to see if President-elect Trump has the skill to be president. And while you watch, Trump and Pence are pulling off one of the most skillfully executed new-CEO moves you will ever see. Remember what I taught you in the past year: Facts don't matter. What matters is how you feel. And when you watch Trump and Pence fight and scratch to keep jobs in this country, it changes how you will feel about them for their entire term. This is a big win for Trump/Pence disguised as a small win.

The political press will dismiss Ford and Carrier with fact-checking. But the stock market will be smarter. Experienced businesspeople recognize the new-CEO move and they know how powerful and important it is.

If you are worried about Trump's talent for leadership, this should help set your mind at ease. He hasn't even started the job and he's already performing better than any past president in the same phase.

The best leaders are the ones who understand human psychology and use that knowledge to address the public's top priorities. For example, investors need optimism about the future to justify investments, and Trump brought optimism about the economy, punctuated by his new-CEO move.

Foreign adversaries need to know America is decisive and willing to use force if needed, and Trump brought that as well. Soon after becoming president, Trump ordered a Tomahawk-missile attack on Syria for its alleged use of chemical weapons. You might say that was a new-CEO move specific to the job of commander in chief.

See the pattern?

Trump got the big stuff right while his perma-critics were left to complain about his low approval ratings, his "risky" style, his strongman vibe, his Twitter habits, and maybe some kind of sketchy Russian connection—that sort of thing.

Keep an eye out for the new-CEO move at your workplace, and sometimes in government. When you see it executed right, optimism is warranted. Even if the critics miss the show.

THE MAKING OF A HYPNOTIST

Hypnosis is a special form of persuasion, generally involving one hypnotist guiding one patient (or subject) toward some sort of personal improvement. You don't need to be a trained hypnotist to be persuasive, but understanding what hypnosis can and cannot do is extraordinarily valuable. It can change your entire worldview. That's what happened to me when I trained to be a hypnotist. I once believed people use facts and reason to make decisions. When I disagreed with people, I assumed it was because I had different facts or better reasons.

That was an illusion.

The reality one learns while practicing hypnosis is that we make our decisions first—for irrational reasons—and we rationalize them later as having something to do with facts and reason. If you believe humans are fundamentally rational, you will have a hard time learning to be a hypnotist because hypnotists rely on our *irrational* brain wiring to persuade. The most effective politicians do the same. In this chapter I'll give you some background on hypnosis to show you how easily the human mind can be rewired by a skilled operator. This background will help you understand Trump's election victory, and it might explain a lot of other mysteries in your personal and professional life.

I've been interested in hypnosis since I was a child. My family doctor was a hypnotist, and he hypnotized my mother to eliminate her pain when she gave birth to my sister. My mother said that although she was hypnotized—or so she claimed—she was conscious of the entire birth process and felt no discomfort. And that was without pain meds, at least according to my mom.

In hindsight it's not clear how much of that story was true. One of the things I've learned as a lifelong student of persuasion is that false memories are common. And sometimes adults don't tell the truth. My mother was a straight shooter, so I doubt she made up the story. But I can't be sure she remembered everything accurately, such as whether or not someone actually gave her pain meds and she forgot that part.

In any event, I bought into my mother's story, and I vowed to someday learn this thing called hypnosis. I hoped that learning hypnosis would imbue me with some sort of superpower.

It turns out I was right.

When I was in my midtwenties, living in San Francisco, I signed up for an evening class at the Clement School of Hypnosis. (It no longer exists.) And by "school" I mean there were about ten students learning from one professional hypnotist. If I recall, we met twice a week for about ten weeks, or something along those lines. The instructor hypnotized the class a number of times so we could experience hypnosis from the receiving side. After he taught us enough technique, we practiced on one another and—for homework—we hypnotized willing strangers and reported back on our progress.

I know you want me to teach you how to be a hypnotist. But you can't learn it from a book. Some skills require a lot of in-person practice, and this is one of them. Part of the process of learning hypnosis involves building confidence in your skills until your subjects can sense it by your demeanor. That confidence is a key ingredient to making hypnosis work. You can build up to that confidence in a class setting, over time, in a way that I doubt anyone can get from a book. If you try a method from a book and it doesn't work on the first try, you'll probably dismiss the book as a scam and stop trying. Learning hypnosis from a book *might* be possible, but I've never heard of anyone pulling it off.

PERSUASION TIP 9

Display confidence (either real or faked) to improve your persuasiveness. You have to believe yourself, or at least appear as if you do, in order to get anyone else to believe.

Hypnosis is largely an observational skill. Half of the process involves looking for microchanges in the subject so you can determine whether or not the approach you are using is having the effect you want. You can't get good at an observational skill without lots of practice. A subject under hypnosis has a distinctive look that I doubt I could describe in words, and I'm good at describing things in words. But the look of a hypnotized subject is unmistakable once you have seen it often enough. You can't get that sort of experience from a book. You have to observe a lot of people under hypnosis to recognize it.

I found it easy to get volunteers for hypnosis by saying I was enrolled in a hypnosis class. I doubt I could have recruited volunteers so easily by saying I was reading a book about hypnosis. The class gave me some credibility with strangers, and a hypnotist in training

PERSUASION TIP 10

Persuasion is strongest when the messenger is credible.

needs a lot of strangers to practice on. One of the things we learned in class is that hypnotizing friends and family doesn't work well because you have too much history and baggage to overcome. People close to you will have trouble getting into the mind-set that you suddenly have a magical new skill. Strangers are more likely to grant you the assumption of credibility, even if you are only a student of hypnosis. And you need the credibility for the hypnosis to work.

One of the most confusing things about hypnosis is that the things you think it *can* do, it probably can't. But the things you *didn't* know it could do—such as predicting presidential outcomes—are mind-boggling.

I spoke to a number of other trained persuaders during the election. The following observation is purely anecdotal, but I don't recall any trained persuaders thinking Clinton was a lock to win. Most predicted an outright Trump win, or at least a surprisingly close race.

You've probably heard of people using hypnosis to lose weight or to stop smoking cigarettes. Hypnosis works for those methods about as well as other nonmedical methods—and by that I mean it usually doesn't work. People who go on diets usually fail no matter what method they use. People who try to stop smoking also fail more often than not.

Hypnosis gets you about the same poor result as other nonmedical methods.

The reason hypnosis is not a powerful tool for losing weight or quitting smoking is almost humorously simple: You *don't want* to eat less and you *don't want* to stop smoking. Smokers and overeaters like both of those things. That's the whole problem. If people didn't enjoy eating and smoking, they wouldn't be doing those things. And hypnosis is only good for getting you what you *do want*. If any part of your mind doesn't fully embrace the change you want, hypnosis might be the wrong tool.

But hypnosis can work well in situations where the subject has no objection to modifying an old behavior. For example, let's say you want to overcome a specific type of fear. In those cases, the subject has zero desire to keep the fear. The fear provides no pleasure or other benefit. Hypnosis can work well in those situations. But you are still fighting against some sort of irrational wiring in the subject's mind, so success is not guaranteed with hypnosis. Every brain is different, and every hypnotist is different.

The best situation for hypnosis is when there is no precondition to overcome. Preconditions in this context might include an irrational fear, a love of eating junk food, or an addiction to smoking. Those cases are hard because some part of your mind wants to keep the old behavior.

But sometimes you are working toward a change that has no precondition to overcome, and that's the best situation. For example, if you were already a well-adjusted person and you wanted to learn how to relax more effectively, hypnosis would be a great tool. In this case, there is no objection to relaxing—the person just doesn't have the tools to do it well. Hypnosis can provide the right tools.

It might also surprise you that a hypnotist can sometimes induce massive orgasms in a willing subject just by choosing the right words in a private setting. But that won't work unless the hypnotist and the subject have some sort of chemistry and a shared desire for that outcome. I know this is possible only because a coworker asked me about it while I was in hypnosis school. At the time, I didn't know if such a thing was possible. But I needed the practice, and she volunteered to be my test subject, so I gave it a try. After about one hour of hypnosis and twenty or so screaming orgasms—no touching involved—she declared the experiment a success. I later learned that the experiment is repeatable with the right kind of subject. That's what I mean by "mind-boggling" power. The point of the story is that hypnosis is a powerful tool when it is working in the same direction as people's existing urges.

You'll be happy to know that hypnosis can't make people do things they know to be wrong in their waking state. Or at least there are no credible stories of that happening. That makes sense to anyone who has ever been hypnotized. A hypnotized person is actually conscious and aware but deeply relaxed. They can open their eyes and walk out the door at any time.

The public has a distorted impression of hypnosis because of movies. In a movie you can hypnotize someone to become an assassin. In real life, that's not possible. In the movies you often see the hypnotist waving a watch or some other pendant-type object and telling you to stare at it. No trained hypnotist does that in real life. It doesn't have a purpose.

By now you are wondering if stage hypnosis is real or just a trick. Stage hypnotists seem to make people do embarrassing things in public, and that would appear to violate what I just said about people not doing things while under hypnosis that they would object to if awake. In the case of stage hypnosis, there is a magic trick involved on top of the hypnosis. The magic trick is that you assume the people onstage think the way you think. If you would be embarrassed doing what you see them doing, you assume they feel the same. But they don't. In any crowd of a hundred people it is easy to find several who are good subjects for hypnosis and also not easily embarrassed by public displays of silliness. The illusion for the audience is that the subjects onstage are so deeply under the hypnotist's spell that they are acting against their own self-interest by embarrassing themselves in public. The secret to the illusion is that the only people who will go onstage in that situation are the ones who know they won't be bothered by the experience.

Further deepening the stage-hypnosis illusion is the fact that many of the subjects are introverts and wallflowers in normal life. But keep in mind that many famous performers are introverts in person and yet have no trouble performing to large crowds. People come in all types. If the stage hypnotist has a large enough audience, you can be sure there are some people who will be comfortable doing silly things onstage. Yes, the subjects *are* hypnotized. But that alone wouldn't be enough to make an unwilling person do embarrassing things in public. The willingness has to be there from the start.

I used a hypnosis technique in the paragraph before last that starts with "By now you are wondering . . ." The hypnosis technique involves demonstrating that I know what you are thinking at the moment you are thinking it. If I guess right, this creates a little bond between the author and the reader because it feels like I know you as well as I might know a friend. It's like I'm in your head. That type of personal connection makes whatever I write seem more interesting to you because you naturally care more about a friend than a stranger.

Hypnotists use the same method to create a quick connection with the subject. If I tell you what you are thinking at the exact moment you are thinking it, I can create the illusion that our minds are somehow connected. And once connected, and comfortable with the connection, the subject is more likely to let the hypnotist later operate the controls.

In my example above, I know from years of experience that when I start to describe hypnosis, it almost always triggers a specific question: "Is stage hypnosis real?" A nonpersuader might provide the answer when asked. But as a trained persuader, I take it one step further and tell you directly that *I know that question is in your head* at the moment that it is. If the question is *not* in your head, you won't even notice that I said it was. You will see my statement as nothing but an introduction to the point. But if I accurately guess that you have curiosity about stage hypnosis, and I answer your unspoken thought at the moment you have it, we form a mental bond that helps you enjoy my writing more. I use that technique to make my writing more personal and powerful. If my writing style seems different from the norm, that's one reason why.

For more tips on writing, I include in appendix B my brief viral blog post on how to be a better writer.

PERSUASION TIP 11

Guess what people are thinking—at the very moment they think it—and call it out. If you are right, the subject bonds to you for being like-minded.

WHO CAN BE HYPNOTIZED?

I often hear people say they "can't be hypnotized" because they tried it once and nothing happened. In my experience—which happens to match what I learned in hypnosis class—an experienced hypnotist can hypnotize anyone, so long as the subject is willing. Where the confusion comes in is that only about 20 percent of the public can experience what hypnotists sometimes call "the phenomena." The term describes any situation in which the subject experiences a full-blown illusion, such as seeing something that isn't there or feeling something that isn't real. My mother's experience of feeling no pain during childbirth falls into that category.

But the 80 percent of the public who can't experience the phenomena can still get tremendous benefits from hypnosis. If you want to learn how to relax, how to be comfortable in a particular situation, or how to perform better at something, the only requirement is that you be willing to be hypnotized. That's good enough for most purposes.

Nonhypnotists are often under the impression that the best subjects for hypnosis are gullible, dumb, or somehow weak-minded. We learned in hypnosis class that there is no personality trait that predicts how easily someone can be hypnotized. Anecdotally, smart people seem to be the easiest to hypnotize. My hypnosis instructor said he thought that was the case, based on experience, and I've noticed the same thing. If there is a correlation with intelligence, it probably has to do with the fact that smart people are less concerned that the hypnotist will turn them into an assassin or a sex slave because they know that isn't a real risk. But as a general rule, there is no way to deduce from a person's intelligence or personality whether that person will be an especially good subject for hypnosis. A trained hypnotist can tell rather quickly how good a subject will be as soon as the process starts, just by watching how the body reacts to suggestions. But there is generally no way to know ahead of time how good a subject will be. And the subjects themselves have no way to know either, but they usually think they do. That's an illusion caused by their egos. People who view themselves as strong willed also imagine they can't be hypnotized. Submissive personality types often assume they will be good subjects for hypnosis. But those variables are not predictive. They just feel as if they should be.

HYPNOSIS SUPERPOWERS

When I signed up for hypnosis class, I assumed I would use the skill I learned only to perform hypnosis on willing subjects. But it turns out that the biggest benefit of learning hypnosis is what it does to your worldview, and how it influences all of your decisions from that point on. Once you see with your own eyes the power of persuasion, and how easily people can be reprogrammed, it changes everything you do.

For example, if you are familiar with my *Dilbert* comic strip, you might know that Dilbert has no last name. His boss has no name at all. You don't know the name of Dilbert's company or what industry it is in. You also don't know its location. All of that omission is intentional. It is a trick I learned from hypnosis class. I leave out any details that would cause readers to feel they are different from the characters in the comic. If Dilbert had a last name, it might tell you something about his ancestry. If you knew for sure that Dilbert's background differed from your own in some big way, it could be an irrational trigger to make you feel less connected. Likewise, if you knew Dilbert's company was in a specific industry that was different from yours, you might feel less connected. By intentionally omitting those details in the design of the *Dilbert* comic, I make it easier for people to think, *Dilbert's job is just like mine.*

> **PERSUASION TIP 12**
>
> If you want the audience to embrace your content, leave out any detail that is both unimportant and would give people a reason to think, *That's not me.* Design into your content enough blank spaces so people can fill them in with whatever makes them happiest.

Lie Detection

An unexpected benefit of learning hypnosis is that I can detect lies with freaky accuracy. Liars usually have "tells," or clues to signal deception. Some of the tells are in the form of body language and facial microchanges—the same things that a hypnotist learns to detect. Liars also use predictable patterns of language that you can pick up once you know what to look for.

For example, if you accuse an *innocent* person of a crime, the accused generally responds by immediately denying the accusation and asking what is wrong with you for even asking. But the first reaction of guilty people, usually, is to ask what evidence you have. They need to know what you know so they can either double down on the lie or confess. Liars confess only if the evidence against them is airtight.

Romance

You can't make someone love you if the chemistry isn't there. Hypnosis isn't that kind of power. But if you have natural chemistry with a person and simply want things to go as well as possible, a working knowledge of hypnosis is immensely useful.

Here I'm not talking about a formal induction, in which a hypnotist puts a subject in a so-called trance state. I'm talking only about the knowledge of human nature that you absorb by studying hypnosis. Once you understand people to be irrational 90 percent of the time, you can give up on your old method of using reason and logic to make someone love you. Love, romance, and sex are fundamentally irrational human behaviors, and it helps to see them that way.

For example, a man who thinks humans are rational creatures might try to attract a woman by being extra nice. That seems reasonable because people like nice people more than they like mean people. But seduction-wise, niceness is boring, and nice people are a dime a dozen. Niceness can get you only so far.

A far better seduction strategy would involve participating in any kind of coed group activities at which you happen to excel. When you display any kind of talent, it triggers other humans to want to mate with you. We're biologically hardwired to be attracted to anything that helps the gene pool, and talent is a signal for valuable genes. So instead of being nice, focus on being talented, or attractive, or smart, or muscular, or something that suggests you have good genes.

A common misconception is that because nice guys seem to finish last and jerky guys seem to get the women, being a jerk must have some sort of seduction advantage. It doesn't. That's an illusion caused by the fact that people who have *other* advantages—such as wealth or beauty—have the freedom to act like jerks because they can attract mates no matter what. If you don't understand what motivates people at a deep level, you might be fooled by your observation that jerks often do well in romance. If being mean were useful to getting sex, you would see ugly people doing it more often with great success. But keep your eyes open and you'll notice that attractive people can get away with being mean, and ugly people can't. Attractiveness is the key correlation.

The exception to this rule is something called "negging" in the language of so-called pickup artists. The idea is to say something subversively negative (negging)—but not too negative—to a woman to make her less confident. For example, the man might walk up to the woman and ask, "Did you just get your hair done?" Notice that it isn't a compliment and it isn't an insult. But the woman will register it as a criticism because there was no compliment appended to the question. The normal structure of that question would be "Did you do something with your hair today? It looks great." When you put the compliment in the question, you're using the "nice" strategy that won't get you far. When you leave out the compliment and ask if the hair is *different* today, it suggests that perhaps you are not crazy about it. That unspoken put-down causes some women (not all, obviously) to reframe their situation as a confident male talking to a woman with some unspoken defect. That creates the illusion—or at least the possibility—that the man is a higher social rank. The perceived difference in social rank—illusion though it is—triggers attraction in the woman in this example because we are biologically wired to believe that people of higher rank probably have some sort of genetic advantage that got them there. And we want to mate with those people to pass those genes to the kids.

Personally, I have never used negging to attract a woman. By the time I learned of the concept, I was already rich and successful, so I had enough perceived status that I didn't need any tricks. You can reach your own

THE MAKING OF A HYPNOTIST 81

conclusions about the ethics of negging. I'm only including it here for education and completeness.

Communicating

After taking the hypnosis class, I became interested in the broader field of persuasion in the normal world. By then I was working at a large bank that encouraged employees to take a variety of in-house classes. I took classes in negotiating, selling, marketing, listening skills, business writing, leadership, public speaking, and more. When you communicate, you are usually trying to persuade, even if you don't see it that way. You might be trying to make someone laugh, persuade someone to buy, cause someone to fall in love or to stay in love. You might be trying to convey talent or knowledge to a professional contact. At a minimum, most communication involves trying to influence people's opinion of *you*, even if the content of your message is neutral. So persuasion and communication overlap quite a bit. If you learn only the tools of communication—the rules of grammar, for example—and you don't learn persuasion, your writing will be weak or, worse, you will make an enormous persuasion mistake and not know it.

A good example of an enormous persuasion mistake happened during the Republican primary debate on September 16, 2015, in Simi Valley, California. Candidate Carly Fiorina tried to cut through the crowded field by graphically describing an alleged video of an abortion that went wrong. (I'm intentionally not describing it here. You'll see why.) When I watched Fiorina's bold move to capture the nation's attention on a key topic for the Republican base, I publicly predicted that she had "self-immolated." I called it the worst persuasion move you are likely to see in any realm. CNN's poll put Fiorina at 15 percent during the week of the debate. As I predicted, she dropped to 4 percent one month later and was soon out of the race.[1]

If you are not a student of persuasion, you might think Fiorina's strategy was bold and clever. It guaranteed free attention from both the mainstream media and social media. And it positioned her as the strongest voice on a key election topic. It was unforgettable, and it matched the emotions of the Republican base. All of that sounds good.

But here's what she got wrong. And this is more wrong than anything you are likely to see in any realm of life, much less politics: *Fiorina paired her brand with a dead baby.*

I knew voters wouldn't want to think about Fiorina's horrible story of a dead baby for one second longer than they needed to. I doubt anyone consciously interpreted the situation as I describe it. But humans don't make political decisions for rational reasons anyway. The Persuasion Filter says Fiorina lost support because she polluted her brand beyond redemption by associating it with the most horrible image one could ever imagine, on live television. If you asked the voters who abandoned Fiorina to give reasons for their switch, they would probably tell you—and they would believe it to be true—that they switched candidates for rational reasons. But according to the Persuasion Filter, they would be rationalizing their irrational decisions without knowing it.

FINDING A HYPNOSIS SCHOOL

By now some of you are wondering how you can find a hypnosis school of your own. (See how I anticipated your question, or at least some people's question?) Unfortunately, I can't help you on this question because I have experience with only one hypnosis school and it no longer exists. If you find a hypnosis school locally, be sure to ask for references from past students. But be skeptical of the references for two reasons:

The school will connect you only with students they know will say good things.

A good hypnotist could give students the impression they got more value than they did.

But don't worry too much about that second point. You wouldn't want to learn hypnosis from an instructor who couldn't persuade his own class to give him good reviews.

PART 3

HOW PRESIDENT TRUMP DOES WHAT OTHERS CAN'T

THE TIME OF KINGS

The following story appeared in my blog on September 4, 2015. I wrote it to make a point about the power of persuasion throughout history. I took some creative license with the historical details, but I stand behind the persuasion points.

This is just for fun, and to prime you for the chapters to come. Take note of how it makes you feel.

Everything that follows is true.

As far as I know.

Centuries ago, in the time of kings, a young autodidact discovered the linguistic interface to the human mind. Some say he was the first wizard. This we cannot know for sure.

The source of the wizard's power was a simple discovery. He learned that when he described to people better versions of themselves, they automatically rewired their minds to rise to his description. At first the wizard used his method to control one person at a time. Before long, he learned how to move entire crowds.

And then he was dangerous.

News of the wizard's power spread across the kingdom. The king dispatched his soldiers to hunt down the wizard and kill him before the wizard's power grew to rival his own.

But it was too late.

The wizard had anticipated his own death. Working feverishly, the wizard managed to condense all he had learned into four words. But there was a risk of leaving those four words and their immense power in the wrong hands after the wizard's death. The world was not ready.

The wizard wrote his four words on scrolls and ordered his people to hide them in a maze of less important words. The wizard hoped that someday a new wizard would find the hidden words and unpack their meaning. And he hoped that by then the world would be ready for such power.

Centuries passed. The words survived, but no wizard came to unlock their true meaning. Many pretenders tried. Wars were fought in an effort to understand the four words and the decoy words surrounding them. It was futile. The words were hidden too well, in plain sight, as wizards do.

Hundreds of years later, in another kingdom, five wizards rose. All of them started life as bright, curious autodidacts. Individually, each of them decoded the hidden message from the original wizard and unlocked the power of the four words.

History does not tell us why five wizards suddenly rose at once, and in the same kingdom. We know only that it happened.

Armed with the power of the four words from the original wizard, each of the wizards amassed fame and power. And each started to notice the unusual successes of the others.

One of the wizards was deeply unattractive. Yet he had the power to seduce any woman.

That is a tell. (A signal.)

One wizard lived like a rich man despite having no net wealth.

That is a tell.

One wizard could inspire men to great acts, using words alone.

That is a tell.

The wizards met one another and shared their secrets. They were good people, by the standards of the day, but their powers caught the attention of the king. Men with so much power were a risk to the throne. So the king raised an army to move against the five wizards.

The five wizards heard of the king's plan and combined forces to defend against his army. The ugly wizard was dispatched to seduce the king of another great power and persuade him to fight on their side. The wizard succeeded. But it wasn't enough.

Another wizard used his powers to raise an army of passionate men who would fight and die for the wizards' cause.

The remaining wizards manipulated the opinions of civilians and raised money to support the war.

The wizards knew their odds of survival were low. So they followed the example of the original wizard and created a linguistic maze to hide their secrets until future wizards could unlock their power.

The five wizards condensed the original wizard's four-word linguistic code down to three *new* words that were a better fit for the times. And they buried the three words in a dense document where none but a future wizard would find them.

Against all odds, the five wizards and their legions of followers prevailed in a long, bloody conflict against the king's forces. After the war, the wizards lived to very old ages, as wizards sometimes can, and passed peacefully.

The words created by the five wizards changed the world in their time and continue to be the most important code in the operating system of human beings. Those three words have toppled dictators, moved mountains, and fed the hungry.

Perhaps someday a future wizard will improve on the code left behind by the five wizards. But I doubt it, because I believe you will never see three more beautiful or powerful words.

Turn the page to see the three words.

"We the People . . ."

The original wizard's four-word code still survives as well. And it has escaped its linguistic maze to join less important words from popular culture. But no matter how many words you put around the original four, none can change its meaning. The four words, in their time, told us of our better selves.

The four words are on the following page.

"Turn the other cheek."

PRESIDENT TRUMP'S TALENT STACK

In my book *How to Fail at Almost Everything and Still Win Big,* I talk about the concept of a talent stack. A talent stack is a collection of skills that work well together and make the person with those skills unique and valuable. For example, a computer programmer who also knows how to do good user interface design would be more valuable than one who does not. The power of the talent stack idea is that you can intelligently combine ordinary talents together to create extraordinary value. The key concept here is that *the talents in the stack work well with one another.* If you acquire the right *combination* of ordinary talents, you don't need to be the world's best at any of them.

For example, I am not a great artist, and I have never taken a traditional class in writing. I'm not the funniest person in my social circle, and I'm not a great business mind either. But few people in the world have a complete talent stack as valuable as mine. By being good enough in each of those individual talents, I can be a famous syndicated cartoonist and enjoy an ideal career. Whenever you see people succeeding beyond your expectations, look for the existence of a well-engineered talent stack.

Case in point: Few people thought Donald Trump would win the presidency in 2016. Part of the reason for that wrongness is that people don't understand the power of persuasion. Trump is the best persuader I've ever seen. A big reason for his persuasion effectiveness is that he has accumulated a remarkable talent stack. If you were to look at any *one* of his talents, you would not be impressed. And that's what fooled observers when they were evaluating his chances. They saw a candidate who was not extraordinarily good at anything in particular. He wasn't the smartest person in the race. He wasn't the most experienced. He wasn't the best communicator (in traditional terms.) For more than half of the country, he wasn't even *likable*. But it didn't matter. What he did have is one of the best talent stacks you will ever see. The combination of his skills is truly special. Let's take a look at President Trump's talent stack.

Publicity: Donald Trump understands the value of publicity, and he knows how to get it. He has spent decades creating controversies and attracting attention to himself and the Trump brand. He isn't the best publicity expert in the world, but most people would agree he's very good.

Reputation: Trump has carefully nurtured a reputation as a business-person who knows how to get things done. His reputation serves him well whenever he enters a new field. His track record makes people feel optimistic about his chances, and that gives him an advantage. People expect him to do well in the future because he has done well in the past. This sort of reputation doesn't happen on its own. Trump has used his skill to create that reputation. You might call it "branding."

Strategy: Trump probably isn't the best strategic thinker in the world. But obviously he is good at making strategic decisions. We saw lots of examples during the election, including his decision to use social media more than a traditional advertising approach. He also campaigned more than Hillary Clinton in the swing states that ended up making all the difference. In hindsight, his strategy was solid.

Negotiating: Trump literally wrote the book on negotiating, called *The Art of the Deal*. Actually, his coauthor, Tony Schwartz, wrote most of it. But obviously it reflected Trump's negotiating preferences.

Persuasion: Trump is the best persuader I have ever seen. But much of that effectiveness is related to his total talent stack. His mastery of the tools of persuasion is fairly ordinary. You will learn most of those tools in this book.

Public speaking: Trump is an entertaining and provocative public speaker, but no one would say he is the world's best orator. He's far better than average, and that's good enough for the talent stack.

Sense of humor: Trump has a good sense of humor, and that's a powerful tool of persuasion. A sense of humor makes people like you, and it makes you look smarter. Trump isn't as funny as professional humorists, but he's funny enough.

Quick on his feet: It's not easy to look relaxed and mentally sharp in public, when all eyes are on you. But it is something you can learn. Trump probably has some natural talent and mental quickness, but when you add to that all of his practice at being a public figure, it's a strong talent.

Thick skinned: Trump's critics like to label him "thin-skinned" because he often attacks his critics. But counterattacking is good persuasion. It tells people that being his friend is better than being his critic. So while Trump looks thin-skinned on the 2-D checkerboard, he's actually super hardened against criticism because he has endured a lifetime of it. When he ran for president, he had to know the abuse would be ten times worse than anything he had experienced before then. You don't sign up for that kind of abuse unless you know you can handle the shaming. Evidently, Trump can. It's a valuable skill, and one you can learn.

High energy: The best persuaders bring the most energy to the topic. Our brains interpret high energy as competence and leadership (even when it isn't). Trump has a natural high energy, and he never lets you forget it.

Size and appearance: Trump is tall, and we humans are primed—by biology and our sexist society—to see tall male figures as leaders. Trump also has a distinctive look, with his stern face and his unusual haircut. His physicality makes him more persuasive both because of his size and because you can't stop looking at his hair. The things you remember and think about the most rise in importance in your mind. One look at Trump in his business suit, with his height, his stern expression, and his unusual haircut, tells you he's important. And Trump knows branding, so he never let us see him in casual clothing during the campaign for president.

Smart: As far as I can tell, Trump is far smarter than the average citizen. On top of that, he has deep experience across a number of different fields, so his intelligence is well rounded.

Trump's talent stack is so strong that I believe he could make almost any basket of policies sound good to the public. I will go so far as to say that Trump could have run as a Democrat, embraced Bernie Sanders's entire platform, and won the election that way.

The popular interpretation of how Trump won is that he understood the American people and devised policies that they wanted. My filter says the opposite. It says Trump convinced the public that his policies were the ones they should care about the most. And so they did. Obviously every voter is different, and one variable doesn't explain an election. But my point is that persuasion was more important to the outcome than policies; we just perceive it to be the other way around.

Remember the two important elements of filters. They should make you happy, and they should do a good job of predicting the future. My filter predicted that Trump would soften his hard-line positions on a number of topics once he got into the general election. And he did. He even went so far as to reverse the key policy platform that got him nominated; he went from a position of mass deportation of undocumented immigrants to one in which he wants to deport only the ones who committed additional crimes after entering the country. At one point he said in an interview that women who get illegal abortions should be punished. The very next day he reversed his position. At one point he talked about punishing the families of terrorists, but that idea went away too.

If you think Trump's policies got him elected, you have to explain why his positions substantially changed during the campaign and he still won. My filter explains it perfectly: Trump is so persuasive that policies didn't matter. People voted for him even as his policies were murky and changing.

Another filter on the election says Trump won because he was the change candidate, and the change candidate has an advantage. But all of the Republican candidates represented a huge change from the Obama presidency. And prior to election day, few experts were predicting that Trump's message of change would win.

I remind you that filters are not intended as windows to reality. Our brains did not evolve to understand reality. We're all running different movies in our heads. All that matters is whether or not your filter keeps you happy and does a good job of predicting. In my experience, the Persuasion Filter does both of those things better than the alternatives.

TRUMP'S ROSIE O'DONNELL MOMENT

As the election started getting traction in all of our minds, in the summer of 2015, I was experimenting with a new comic that featured a talking robot that never moves. He just reads the news. You can see in this comic that I had already noticed Trump's successful use of persuasion that was confusing the public.

But I didn't know how big a deal this was until what I now call the "Rosie O'Donnell Moment." In the first Republican debate, on August 6, 2015, Megyn Kelly was moderating, and her first question to Trump should have ended his campaign on the spot. Only a few people in the world could have escaped her trap.

Kelly started to frame her dangerous question by saying, "You've called women you don't like 'fat pigs,' 'dogs,' 'slobs,' and 'disgusting animals...'"

Trump interrupted her by saying, "Only Rosie O'Donnell."

Kelly finished her question and Trump responded with something about the problem of political correctness. But by then it didn't matter. The Rosie O'Donnell reference sucked all the energy out of the room. It was a masterstroke of persuasion, timed perfectly, and executed in front of the world. When I saw it happen, I stood and walked toward the television (literally). I got goose bumps on my arm. *This wasn't normal.* This was persuasion like I have never seen it performed in public. And in that moment, I saw the future unfold. Or I thought I did. It would take another year to be sure.

HOW A MASTER PERSUADER MOVES ENERGY AND FOCUS

What made Trump's Rosie O'Donnell response so masterful? For starters, consider how a normal, mainstream politician would have handled that trap. Most would have stated positive things about women and tried to change the subject. But that would be a failing strategy because there was so much public record of Trump's past statements about women. It would just keep coming back.

Trump didn't answer the way anyone expected. Trump used his weapons-grade persuasion and stacked together several techniques in a few sentences.

He created an **emotion-triggering visual image** (Rosie O'Donnell) that sucked all the attention from the question to the answer, and it wasn't even a real answer. Our visual sense is the most persuasive of our five senses, so using a real person whom we recognize, and can imagine, is a great technique. He also picked a personality who was sure to trigger the emotions of his base. Republicans generally don't like Rosie O'Donnell because of her outspoken liberal views.

Trump knew his Republican base has a strong negative reaction to O'Donnell, so he bonded with them on that point. This is the persuasion method known as **pacing and leading.** First you match your audience's emotional condition to gain trust, and later you are in a position to lead them.

Trump also used the **High-Ground Maneuver** by taking the question out of the weeds of what he said in the past and up to the concept of how much it hurts the world to be bound by such silly political correctness. I'll tell you more about the High-Ground Maneuver in its own chapter.

Trump guaranteed that all media attention would be on him because the Rosie O'Donnell quote is simply too interesting (and funny) to ignore. He sucked all the attention away from his sixteen competitors, rendering them uninteresting by comparison. That never changed.

None of this looked like luck to me. It was pitch-perfect technique, and it leveraged most of his *persuasion talent stack*, either directly or indirectly. Trump's response to Kelly was funny, strategic, smart, memorable, visually persuasive, thick skinned (he didn't seem bothered), provocative, and perfectly on brand. He converted Kelly's attack into pure energy and then moved that energy where it suited him best. Normal people can't do that. They wouldn't even know how to start. When I saw it live, I realized it wasn't business as usual. This was something special.

Inspired by what I saw at the debate, I wrote a blog post that became one of the most viral things I have written. The post was titled "Clown Genius." It was my first step in reframing Trump as a Master Persuader. But I couldn't directly jump into my main point. First I had to pace my readers—by agreeing with their way of thinking about candidate Trump. Once I established that trust and credibility, I started to lead them to a new way of viewing Trump's capabilities.

Posted August 13, 2015

Like many of you, I have been entertained by the unstoppable clown car that is Donald Trump. On the surface, and several layers deep as well, Trump appears to be a narcissistic blowhard with inadequate credentials to lead a country.

The only problem with my analysis is that there is an eerie consistency to his success so far. Is there a method to it? Is there some sort of system at work under the hood?

That was the pacing part of my persuasion. Next I described Trump's escape from the Rosie O'Donnell trap, as I have again in this chapter. I expected readers to agree with me that Trump did an unusually good job of escaping the trap. With that pacing behind me, I could lead my readers even further. Here is what I said.

You probably cringed when Trump kept saying his appearance gave Fox its biggest audience rating. That seemed totally off point for a politician, right? But see what happened.

Apparently Fox News chief Roger Ailes called Trump and made peace. And by that I mean Trump owns Fox News for the rest of the campaign, because his willingness to appear on their network will determine their financial fate. *Bam*, Trump owns Fox News and paid no money for it. See how this works? That's what a strong brand gives you.

You probably also cringed when you heard Trump say Mexico was sending us their rapists and bad people. But if you have read this far, you now recognize that intentional exaggeration as an anchor, and a standard method of persuasion.

You will learn more about anchors later in this book.

On a recent TV interview, the host (I forget who) tried to label Trump a "whiner." But instead of denying the label, Trump embraced it and said he was the best whiner of all time, and the country needs just that. That's a psychological trick I call "taking the high ground." The low ground in this case is the unimportant question of whether "whiner" is a fair label for Trump. But Trump cleverly took the high ground, embraced the label, and used it to set an anchor in your mind that he is the loudest voice for change. That's some clown genius for you.

Persuasion isn't the most predictive variable in every situation. Life is generally messy and complicated, with lots of powerful influences at play. But a presidential debate is not that messy and not that complicated. It is an artificial situation created for the purpose of limiting the number of variables. In that environment, a Master Persuader can rule, and a trained observer can see the technique as it happens. That's what made the Rosie O'Donnell moment so compelling to me. Megyn Kelly challenged the greatest persuader of our generation to show his stuff to the world, free of external distractions and variables. And when he did, I saw the future unfold.

THE PERSUASION STACK

Some forms of persuasion are stronger than others. Here I am talking about the broad categories of persuasion and not the specific tools. Below I rank for you the broad forms of persuasion by their relative power. The strongest are at the top. Notice that the emotional topics near the top are stronger than the more "rational" ones at the bottom. This is based entirely on my own experience as a persuader. The persuasion stack isn't science, so I recommend viewing it as directional.

- Big fear
- Identity
- Smaller fear
- Aspirations
- Habit
- Analogies
- Reason
- Hypocrisy
- Word-thinking

As I will explain in more detail in an upcoming chapter, visual persuasion is stronger than oral persuasion. And most of the persuasion stack can be communicated either way. In practical terms, that means a visual presentation of a weaker form of persuasion could be stronger than a written or oral presentation of something higher in the stack. For example, visual persuasion involving a small fear would normally be more powerful than an academic discussion of a big fear that included no visuals. But if the communication method is the same, my ranking of the persuasion stack generally holds.

I'll take you through the stack, starting with the weakest forms at the bottom.

WORD-THINKING

Word-thinking is a term I invented to describe a situation in which people are trying to win an argument by adjusting the definition of words. In these situations there is no appeal to reason. But that's okay, because facts and logic are not persuasive anyway. Word-thinking usually happens when people are bad at logic but don't realize it. And that's most of us, most of the time. So you see this form of nonthinking more than any other.

The clearest example of word-thinking is the abortion topic. Both sides try to win the debate by declaring their definition of "life" to be the accurate one. Most people agree that protecting human life is among our most important priorities, so if the antiabortion folks can define a fetus as living, they win the debate without resorting to any actual reasons or logic. It is easy to see why people *try* to win debates this way. But the other side is unlikely to change their opinions just because someone adjusted the definition of a word. Word-thinking simply isn't persuasive.

As technology improves, we have to continually reassess what it means for a fetus to be alive. And that makes no sense at all. The current state of technology should make no difference to whether an entity is defined to be living or not. Both sides of the debate agree on what a fetus can and cannot do on its own. If I say the scientific description of a fetus fits my personal definition of what it means to be alive, and you say it does not, there is no place to go with that argument. Our best-case scenario is a tie.

We saw a lot of word-thinking in the presidential race of 2016. At the beginning of the election cycle we saw an ongoing debate about whether Donald Trump was "conservative" enough to be the Republican nominee. The people who said he was not a true conservative were trying to use word-thinking to eliminate Trump from consideration as the Republican candidate. Their problem was that people did not agree on what it meant to be conservative, nor did the public think it was especially important for Trump's talents and policies to map to some underdefined political label. This was the blind spot in the Republican Party that allowed Trump to become their leader without being especially conservative. The entrenched interests in the GOP were doing word-thinking—literally the worst form of persuasion—to protect themselves from a Master Persuader with an enormous stockpile of persuasion weaponry. It was never a fair fight. As a trained persuader, I could see this developing from the start. As long as the Republican establishment clung to word-thinking for their defense, they had no defense at all.

HYPOCRISY

On television news shows these days you often see pundits defending their side of an issue by saying their opponents do the same sorts of bad things, or have in the past. This is a good way to fill television time, and it might add some information to the conversation. But it can never be terribly persuasive to the viewer. The problem is that it frames both parties as naughty children. There are no winners in that framing.

I understand the impulse to cry hypocrisy. You don't want the other side to claim their brand is pure while branding your side as wrongdoers. So you do have to sling back some mud. But the "Your side did it too" response is weak mud. The stronger mud is what I call the High-Ground Maneuver. I talk about this in more detail in the How to Use the High-Ground Maneuver chapter, but you need a sneak peek at the concept now for comparison purposes.

The High-Ground Maneuver involves taking the conversation out of the children-are-bickering mode and reframing it as you—the adult in the room—explaining to the children how things work. Let me give you an example, starting with the weak persuasion of claiming the other side is just as bad.

Hypocrite Accusation

Pundit 1: Your side didn't do enough to end street violence.

Pundit 2: Well, don't forget that your side failed at it too!

Result: Tie. Both sides are bad.

High-Ground Maneuver

Pundit 1: Your side didn't do enough to end street violence.

Pundit 2: I agree. Luckily we have learned a lot since then. A number of cities experimented with different approaches and some worked better than others. Let's try to find the best practices and see if we can spread them to other cities.

Result: Pundit 1 is framed as the child who has nothing to offer but complaints. Pundit 2 demonstrates an adult understanding of how to solve problems over time.

PERSUASION TIP 13

Use the High-Ground Maneuver to frame yourself as the wise adult in the room. It forces others to join you or be framed as the small thinkers.

Notice I started by fully embracing the criticism from the other side. If you debate the criticism, you stay in a child frame. If you accept it and make a case for learning and improving, you move to the adult high ground and leave the children behind. Whenever you see claims of hypocrisy, you are also likely to see an opportunity for the High-Ground Maneuver.

REASON

We humans like to think we are creatures of reason. We aren't.[1] The reality is that we make our decisions first and rationalize them later.[2] It just doesn't feel that way to us. That's why I often said during the 2015–16 election that "facts and policies don't matter." Obviously the facts and policies *do* matter to outcomes. But in terms of persuasion, facts and policies and reason are almost useless.

The exception to this rule is when there is no emotional content to a decision and you have all the information you need. In those cases, we can use our capacity for reason. For example, you might use your sense of reason and your command of the facts to shop for the best price across multiple sellers. As long as you have no emotional investment in the topic, reason and facts can be quite persuasive. Once you remove emotion from the decision, reason and facts are all you have to go on.

But most topics in the real world are emotional. We are emotional about our relationships, our career choices, and our politics. And those topics can influence everything else we do. For example, if you are in a relationship, it is difficult to purchase anything meaningful without considering the emotional impact it will have on your partner. So even our most objective and simple choices acquire emotional dimensions over time because of the people around us.

We're even emotional about our garbage. Consider the campaign that started decades ago to persuade citizens to recycle. The government can persuade some citizens to recycle simply by saying it is good for the planet. But you get more people to comply by making recycling a semipublic process. Visitors to your house will notice that you either have a recycling bin or not. And you can be sure they will judge you accordingly. And neighbors will see your trash and recyclables sitting by the curb in front of your house on trash pickup day. On its surface, the question of recycling is about resource management. That boring topic wouldn't motivate many people to comply. But because recycling is semipublic by its nature, and people don't want to be branded as bad citizens, they recycle when they know they are being watched. People are motivated to avoid social embarrassment.

The social pressure to recycle doesn't end with the neighbors, either. Kids will pester parents to recycle because the kids learned about it in school. So parents are getting the stink eye from every direction when they don't do a good job of recycling. The social pressure to recycle is enormous. But if you ask people *why* they recycle, they will tell you it is good for the planet. They won't tell you they do it to avoid social embarrassment, or to be consistent with their identities as "green" people, or to be good role models for the kids. The recycling example is somewhat typical of how we run the rest of our lives. Sometimes we have access to good data and sometimes we use our limited powers of reason. But data and reason are generally subordinated to how we feel. We tell ourselves—and anyone else who will listen—that we are rational decision makers. But that is largely an illusion.

Your illusion of being a rational person is supported by the fact that sometimes you do act rationally. All the *little* things you do every day are probably rational. You brush your teeth to avoid cavities, you set your alarm clock to wake up on time, and so on. So your daily experience of living involves making one rational decision after another. You also believe— incorrectly—that you are rational when you make the big decisions about love and money and lifestyle. But that's mostly a result of cognitive dissonance and confirmation bias. When we do irrational things—such as marry someone who is obviously a bad choice—we always have plenty of "reasons" to offer. But those reasons are rationalizations. And those rationalizations, along with your experience of being rational on the little decisions, creates for you the illusion that you are rational most of the time, including on the big decisions.

The illusion is helped along by the fact that even your big irrational decisions have plenty of rational thought at their base. For example, if you are looking for love, you probably use your sense of reason to eliminate from your search dead people, people in jail, and animals. You know that none of those approaches is likely to end well. So we do use reason to narrow down our choices. But when it comes to the final decision, our sense of reason takes a long walk while our irrational mind applies our biases, hopes, and fears to the decision. And when we are done with that irrational process, we will explain it to ourselves, and to anyone else who will listen, as a product of our rational thought.

It isn't.

In the early parts of the 2016 presidential election, the media believed that Trump was picking up early support from people who liked his policies, especially his tough stand on immigration. I predicted early in the election that Trump—the Master Persuader—would moderate his policies in the general election and pick up new supporters without losing many of the old ones. This makes no sense if you think facts and policies matter. What mattered was that people saw Trump agree with them on an emotional dimension—that immigration was a big problem that needs fixing. Once he agreed with voters on an emotional level, he was free to tweak the details of his policies, and people followed him. What persuaded people to support Trump was his emotional connection. Trump's policy details evolved over time. If the *details* of the policies mattered to people's decisions, I have a hard time imagining Trump getting elected.

You might have seen a viral video on *Jimmy Kimmel Live* of street interviews in which a prankster presented Trump's policy positions as Hillary Clinton's policies and asked her supporters if they agreed with those positions.[3] Lots of people said they did. I'll take it one step further by saying Trump would have won the election even if he and Clinton had switched positions and erased our memories of their old opinions. It literally didn't matter what policies either person brought to the table. People made up their minds based on biases alone. That is typical when you get to the final two candidates, as both of them are capable of doing the job. So we use our biases to break the tie. Later we will imagine that our reasons were totally rational.

ANALOGIES

Analogies are a good way to explain a new concept. For example, I describe my start-up's app (WhenHub) as being "like the Uber app without the Uber car." And by that I mean any group of friends can stream their locations to one another as they approach a destination on the app's map.

The analogy is only my *starting point* for describing the app. Once I have established the basic concept, I can add details, and the listener has a framework to which they can attach the new information. That's a sensible way to explain a new idea. You can use an analogy to give the listener a memory structure that you then embellish with details.

While analogies are useful and important for explaining new concepts, here's the important point for our purposes: Analogies are *terrible* for persuasion.

PERSUASION TIP 14

When you attack a person's belief, the person under attack is more likely to harden his belief than to abandon it, even if your argument is airtight.

Unfortunately, most people believe that analogies are one of the *best* ways to persuade. That fact goes far in explaining why it seems that every debate on the Internet ends with a Hitler analogy. The phenomenon is so common it has its own name: Godwin's law. But I doubt many people have changed an opinion just because a stranger on the Internet compared them to Hitler. A direct attack usually just hardens people into their current opinions.

There are two good reasons why analogies fail to persuade. The first is that they are a form of pseudologic, much like word-thinking. For people who are unfamiliar with the mechanics of logic and reason, analogies *feel* as if they *should* work. And how can you explain the prevalence of Hitler analogies if they don't persuade? Wouldn't someone have noticed by now?

I can answer those questions.

People are irrational. If something feels as if it *should* work, most of us conclude that it does. We don't have the time or resources to do scientific inquiry on every choice we make. So we use our "common sense" and our "gut feeling" to get by. That's the typical worldview. But the Persuasion Filter says your common sense and gut feelings are little more than magical thinking.

Most of us believe we have common sense. And yet we disagree with one another about what that looks like. That's all you need to know about common sense. The illusion is that you have this thing called common sense and many others do not. The Persuasion Filter takes it one step further and says *no one has common sense.* According to the filter, sometimes we make good choices and sometimes we don't. When things go wrong, we blame the environment or bad luck, or we imagine it was a rare misfire by our common sense. When things turn out in our favor, we believe it is because we have common sense and it served us well. In both cases it is no more than rationalization after the fact.

One of the common views of reality is that we humans can reach good decisions based on some combination of subconscious thoughts and bodily sensations. We like to justify that decision-making process with words such as "hunch," "instinct," and "intuition." The Persuasion Filter says this is just one of the ways we rationalize the awkward fact that we are not using our sense of reason to make decisions. When a decision involves lots of facts, and we have access to all the facts, we are more likely to hallucinate that we used our powers of reason to reach a decision. But when we recognize that we don't have all the facts, we hallucinate that we used our gut feeling to bridge the gap. In both cases we acted irrationally, and we tried to rationalize it to ourselves after the fact. That's how the Persuasion Filter sees it.

The Persuasion Filter does not attempt to explain reality, if there is such a thing. I present it as a useful *filter* for understanding your world and predicting what might happen next. If a filter on reality makes you happy, and it does a good job predicting, that is probably a good filter.

But let's get back to analogies.

As I explained, the first reason analogies fail at persuasion is that they are not designed for that job. Analogies are not logic. They are just a quick way to explain a new concept.

The second reason analogies fail is because they are imprecise by definition. That gives people on the other side of a debate all kinds of ammunition. And no one changes their mind when they have that much ammunition for a defense. As it turns out, all of the ammunition provided by bad analogies is in the form of blanks, because analogies are not persuasive, and neither are the criticisms of analogies. If you are arguing

about the details of an analogy, you are not persuading, and you are not being persuaded. You are just wasting time.

But what about comparing Trump to Hitler? Wasn't that persuasive?

On social media, and sometimes even in the mainstream media, Clinton's supporters relentlessly compared Trump to Hitler. It was brutally effective persuasion when packaged with related accusations about his "temperament" and his strongman vibe. Fear is the strongest level of persuasion, and the Persuasion Filter would say the Hitler-related persuasion made a difference in the election.

You might wonder why I say analogies do not persuade while at the same time I say the comparisons of Trump to Hitler were effective. The answers to that question will take you to a deeper level of understanding about persuasion.

My hypothesis—consistent with the Persuasion Filter—is that people who already had a firm opinion of Trump were not persuaded by the Hitler analogies. That is consistent with analogies being a weak form of persuasion.

But not all voters had a firm opinion of Trump. If you are young, you probably didn't experience much of Trump's personal history as it happened. And if you didn't watch *The Apprentice*, you didn't know him from there either. For the people who didn't already know Trump, the Hitler analogy was effective, not because analogies are persuasive but because this one did a good job *explaining* Trump for the first time to people who had no deep knowledge of him. Remember, analogies are great for *explaining* a new concept. And this concept of Trump as a new Hitler was filling an empty space for lots of voters who didn't know much about Trump. And this brings us to another persuasion topic I have already mentioned: anchors.

HOW TO CREATE MENTAL ANCHORS

The first thing you hear about a new topic automatically becomes an anchor in your mind that biases your future opinions. In the comic above, Dilbert's nemesis got to Dilbert's boss first and told him Dilbert was a liar. That would prime the boss's filter to expect Dilbert to lie, with confirmation bias nearly guaranteeing that he would see things that way in the future.

But if Dilbert had complained to his boss first, Dilbert would maintain his credibility, and whoever called him a liar later would have a tougher sell. In the 3-D world of persuasion, going first makes a big difference.

You see this technique most often from good negotiators. They open with a ridiculously low or ridiculously high offer to bias the other side in that direction. For example, suppose you offered to be my consultant and I have no idea what your services are worth. If the first thing you tell me is that some clients pay you $1,000 per hour, I'm more likely to agree to a higher price than if the first number you told me was $100. The initial number becomes a mental anchor that is hard to move. That's why you should always be the first to offer numbers, even if you are talking about an *entirely different situation.* [Yes, that works. See Robert Cialdini's great book *Pre-Suasion.*]

For example, let's say you are trying to sell your business, and neither you nor your potential buyer knows what it is worth. A business is only as good as its future, and the future is unknown. So there is a lot of bias and guessing involved when anyone buys a one-of-a-kind business. If you are the seller of the business, you want to prime the buyer by mentioning the high price paid by someone else in an *entirely different context.* That's often enough to anchor a person to the high number even though it is a different conversation.

For example, if you would be happy to get $5 million for your company, it might help to have a casual conversation before the negotiations about a billionaire who bought a $25 million yacht. Once the $25 million figure gets into your buyer's head—even though it has nothing to do with the company you are selling—it forms an anchor. And it might help you get a higher price.

When my start-up partners and I were brainstorming how to describe WhenHub.com to investors, we had lots of valid ways to start that description, all based on fact and all totally appropriate and honest. I steered the team toward opening with a comparison of the ways in which WhenHub could be viewed as a new player in the office-suite application space [Word, Excel, PowerPoint, Google Docs, Sheets, and Slides]. Those are multibillion-dollar products. We think WhenHub belongs in that group, sizewise and functionwise. That opening idea anchors investors to the vastness of the opportunity.

Is this sort of framing unethical? It depends on the situation. I wouldn't use this method to negotiate with a family member or friend. But in a business context, you expect both sides to be using commercial-grade persuasion of this sort. And you don't want to go to a gunfight armed only with a knife. In a business negotiation, each side expects at least *some* hyperbole and "selling" technique from the other. Make your own decision about whether it's ethical to use the same persuasion tools your adversaries are using.

In the case of WhenHub, the comparison to office-suite products is entirely appropriate and we back it up. The sneakier form of persuasion would involve talking about recent unicorn start-ups in general before making our pitch, to benefit from any unconscious mental associations. That would be pure persuasion without helpful information, and you can use your judgment on the ethics of it. I wouldn't use it on a friend, but I would use it in a hostage negotiation.

The human brain forms a bias for the things it hears first. If we accept the thing we hear first, it tends to harden into an irrational belief. And then it is difficult to dislodge. If your friends are reinforcing the idea too, it becomes hard as steel.

The Persuasion Filter predicts that people who already had a favorable opinion of Trump would not be persuaded by analogies, including Hitler analogies, no matter how skillfully applied. But for those who didn't yet have a firm opinion of Trump, the Hitler analogy formed an anchor that was hard to move. The details of the analogy were unimportant. All that mattered was the association. And this leads me to my next point: Associations matter more than reason.

The Hitler analogy was effective not because analogies are logical or persuasive but because any *association* of two things is persuasive. If you compare any two things long enough, their qualities start to merge in our irrational minds. The illusion created by analogies is that if two situations have *anything* in common, perhaps they have *lots* in common. Trump has a few things in common with Hitler—as do we all—and that makes some of his critics irrationally believe he will also invade Poland.

Pulling all of this together, analogies are not persuasive on their own. But if the analogy is simply a carrier for a persuasive association—let's say, comparing any strong leader to Hitler—the *association* can be persuasive to some, even while the details of the analogy are ridiculous.

Now watch me summarize this point by using an analogy, because analogies are good at explaining new concepts: If your analogy includes a strong negative association (such as Hitler), you could think of the analogy as a holster and the negative association as a gun. The gun is persuasive. The holster is not.

HABIT

If you want to influence someone to try a new product, it helps to associate it with some part of an existing habit. For example, people usually follow a consistent routine of shaving, showering, makeup, hair, brushing their teeth, etc. The vitamin industry grafted onto that habit when some marketing genius suggested that people should take vitamins once a day. That probably isn't the best way for your body to absorb vitamins and minerals because some of them pass from your body quickly. Biologically speaking, the most effective vitamin-taking schedule would involve multiple doses spread across your day. But if you want to *sell* lots of vitamins, you attach the habit to people's existing get-ready routine—once per day. That makes it stick.

To put it another way, if vitamin companies relied on you to take your vitamins at any random time you liked, it probably wouldn't happen as often as they want. But the early marketers of vitamins cleverly convinced us that taking vitamins fits into our existing waking-up and/or going-to-bed habits. Now the practice of taking vitamins around the same time as you are brushing your teeth seems easy and natural. So we keep doing it.

The makers of the first fitness trackers had habit working for them too. You put your fitness band on your arm as part of your getting-dressed routine in the morning. That helps it stick.

This form of persuasion—grafting onto existing habits—usually isn't helpful for politics because big national topics don't fit into your daily habits. The main way habits come into play for politics is in the way we consume news. So if you wanted to use habit to influence politics, you might call your news program something like *Morning Joe*, which is the name of a show on MSNBC featuring Joe Scarborough and Mika Brzezinski. That tells people it fits into their morning habit.

Habit persuasion is why I started branding my live-streaming on Periscope and YouTube as *Coffee with Scott Adams*. I wanted people to associate my content with their morning coffee, so it became part of their habit.

Based on comments from users, that strategy has been effective. People reported to me that I became part of their morning routine and they missed it when I skipped a day.

Speaking of skipping a day, that reminds me of Persuasion Tip 15.

Now ask yourself whether President Trump

rewards his supporters in a predictable way or in an unpredictable way. Right, he is unpredictable as heck. In the morning he disappoints, but by lunchtime he delights. You never know what is coming. And that, in part, is why his supporters are addicted to him.

ASPIRATIONS

It isn't easy to change people's aspirations, and you would have no reason to try unless the aspirations were somehow harmful or dangerous. But you can improve the power of your persuasion by grafting your story onto people's existing aspirations. You see this a lot in product marketing. For example, Apple tells you that its products will help you be creative. For many people, being more creative is an aspiration. And some financial services companies tell you they will help you be financially independent. That too is an aspiration for most people.

When President Trump was campaigning, he played directly to voter aspirations. He told the unemployed and underemployed that they would someday have good jobs. He told us he would make America safer, richer, and just plain greater, in a variety of ways. That is good aspirational persuasion.

Compare that with Hillary Clinton's campaign slogan about being "Stronger Together." National strength sounds like a good quality to have, but it doesn't feel aspirational. It almost feels defensive. And her main message of being more of the same in terms of being like the Obama administration had no aspirational quality whatsoever. Maintaining a steady course is not an aspiration for people who need help.

Some pundits say Trump won because he was the candidate of change. But not all change is equal. Becoming *stronger together* is a change, but it doesn't speak to our personal aspirations. Trump's theme about jobs speaks directly to aspirational change.

In my opinion, *change* as a stand-alone concept was not a persuasive element in the election. The active part of the persuasion is the change *to what*. Trump offered the more aspirational persuasion.

FEAR (BIG AND SMALL)

Fear can be deeply persuasive. But not all fear-related persuasion is equal. To maximize your fear persuasion, follow these guidelines.

A big fear is more persuasive than a small one.

A personal fear is more persuasive than a generic national problem.

A fear that you think about most often is stronger than one you rarely think about.

A fear with a visual component is scarier than one without.

A fear you have experienced firsthand (such as a crime) is scarier than a statistic.

Both Hillary Clinton and Donald Trump used fear in their campaign persuasion. Trump spoke of the fears of terrorism and crime from undocumented immigrants. Clinton's brand didn't allow her to use those same fears for persuasion, so she cleverly used Trump himself as the object of fear by painting him as a racist, sexist, homophobic, erratic dictator with the nuclear launch codes. Branding Trump as the next Hitler (without using that actual word) was Clinton's most powerful persuasion strategy. Had this been the only variable in the campaign, Clinton would have won.

IDENTITY

If you don't have an opportunity to scare people into doing what you want them to do, the next-strongest technique is an appeal to identity. We saw President Obama win over 90 percent of the African American vote. We saw most women prefer Hillary Clinton to Donald Trump. And so on. People like to back their "tribe" as they see it. And all of us are in multiple tribes if you consider our genders, ethnicities, ages, wealth, religions, political parties, and all the rest. Humans reflexively support their own tribe. No thinking is involved.

This reflex makes sense from an evolutionary perspective. The people on your team were the ones helping to keep you alive. The people on every other team were trying to kill you or take your resources. We evolved to feel safer with, and to generally prefer, people who are similar to us in any substantial way. This instinct to support our own team is the reason major sports are big business. It makes no logical sense to support your local team just because it is local. But we do. It is a reflex.

President Trump used identity persuasion to remind voters that they were Americans first. Clinton used identity persuasion to tell women, minorities, and the LGBTQ community that they were on her team.

The interesting thing about the candidates' identity persuasion is that Clinton stuck with genetic distinctions and Trump did a High-Ground Maneuver by speaking to the way we are socialized (brainwashed) to feel patriotic. There is no way to know which strategy was more persuasive, but both were strong.

The next time someone is doing something you find objectionable, don't attack that person's actions. Instead, ask if this is who the person wants to be. Most people think they are good people, even if they sometimes do bad things. If you remind them of their identity, and their aspirations for their identity, you will usually be met with cognitive dissonance and an implied promise to change. That might look like this:

> **Other person:** "I like defacing the political signs on the other side. Ha-ha! It's hilarious."
>
> **You:** "Is that the person you want to be?"
>
> **Other person (now with cognitive dissonance):** "Um, I was just doing it that one time because I was with Bob, and we had some drinks."

Obviously this method won't work with kids, or with adults who have cultivated a brand around doing all the wrong things. But if you catch a normal adult doing something outside what you imagine is their aspiration of a core identity, you can sometimes flip them to be compatible with their preferred identity almost instantly. Just point out the gap and watch it close.

SETTING THE TABLE

One of the ways I make myself more persuasive is by telling people I'm a trained hypnotist and that I am familiar with all of the tools of influence. I learned in hypnosis class that it is easier to persuade people when they *expect* to be persuaded. If your persuasion skills are viewed as credible, people will persuade themselves that you can persuade them, and that makes everything easier. Credibility, of any sort, is persuasive. That's why doctors and lawyers post their degrees on the wall where everyone can see them. That's why high-end consultants wear expensive business suits. When you signal your credentials, people expect you to have more influence over them. That's how we're wired. We defer to experts almost automatically.

In 1987 Donald Trump's book *The Art of the Deal* became a number one *New York Times* best seller. The book's success told the world that Trump was more than a rich kid who inherited a fortune from Dad. It sent the message that Trump was self-made (to a degree) because of his negotiating talents. And once you convince the world that you are a great negotiator, that version of reality becomes self-fulfilling. It is easier to persuade people when they expect you to be persuasive.

Imagine going into a negotiation against a business adversary who literally wrote the book on negotiating. In some cases, I assume Trump's reputation as a skilled negotiator stiffened the resistance of the people on the other side of the deal. But my educated guess, based on what I know about persuasion, is that Trump's reputation as a negotiator gave his opponents a subconscious form of *permission* to do poorly in negotiating against him. You *expect* the better negotiator to come out ahead, so there is no shame if it happens. Trump has enjoyed that advantage since his book was published. The book is not just *about* persuasion—it *is* persuasion.

> **PERSUASION TIP 16**
>
> It is easier to persuade a person who believes you are persuasive.

I also learned in hypnosis class that it is easier to hypnotize someone who is paying you for the service. And the more the client pays, the easier it is for the hypnotist, because charging a higher price assigns a higher perceived value to your skills. That's why I practiced my hypnosis on paying customers. I ran an ad in a local publication offering to use hypnosis to regress people back to memories of prior lives. Anecdotally, it did seem to me that the paying customers were easier to hypnotize compared with random volunteers. People who are willing to pay money for hypnosis are more motivated, and that makes a big difference. And they assumed my hypnosis skills were commercial grade because they were paying for the experience. That is the ideal setup for persuasion. My subjects wanted and expected to be influenced.

I should mention that I don't believe in reincarnation, although I was open to the idea at the time I was learning hypnosis. Under hypnosis, my paying clients described in detail what they *imagined* were their prior lives. Listening to those manufactured memories—that I intentionally caused—was enough to convince me that people can't really remember prior lives under hypnosis. I came to that conclusion because none of my subjects ever described a prior life that isn't the topic of lots of movies. My subjects tended to "remember" being Native Americans, Egyptian queens, Vikings, and other well-known historical types. No one ever "remembered" a prior life that would be unfamiliar to modern people. And none of my clients said they were Chinese in a prior life, which seems statistically unlikely given that a quarter of the planet is Chinese.

The concept of setting the table for persuasion has a lot of obvious elements, such as dressing for the part and broadcasting your credentials. But there is also a deeper and scarier level that cognitive scientists have discovered. It turns out that you can influence people's future opinions simply by exposing them to cleverly selected images and ideas that are totally unrelated to the topic of your persuasion. The best book on this topic is *Pre-Suasion*, by Robert Cialdini. One of the examples involves showing subjects images of the American flag before following up with political questions. People who saw the flag image became instantly more amenable to Republican positions. This pre-suasion, as Cialdini calls it, doesn't work on every person. But it doesn't need to. When you are persuading large groups, such as potential customers or voters, you might need to move only 5 percent of them to turn loss into victory.

Cognitive scientists have lots of examples of this form of pre-suasion. Many of them are not obvious in terms of how people will respond. I would not have guessed an American flag biases people Republican. And I would not have guessed that exposing people to stories of generosity would make them more generous on unrelated topics just minutes later. But it does.

The best way to think of pre-suasion is that it creates an emotional state that bleeds over from unrelated topics to the topic of your persuasion. If the American flag makes you feel patriotic, and patriotism is more associated in your mind with Republicans (irrationally or not), that's good enough to persuade.

Kids, if you want to persuade your parents to do something nice for you, first show them a YouTube video of someone being nice to their pets. Then change the subject to whatever it is that you want. The emotional state your parents picked up from watching pet-related kindness should rub off and cause them to look more kindly on whatever you are asking them to do for you. Pre-suading, or setting the table, is about creating mental and emotional associations that carry over. If you get the mood right, and your credibility is high, you're halfway done with your persuasion before anyone knows you started.

Here's a checklist you can use to see how well you set the table for your own future persuasion. Make sure you . . .

❑ Dress for the part. If you dress like a knowledgeable professional, people will assume your opinions and advice are credible. That makes it easier to persuade.

❑ Improve your physical appearance via diet, exercise, hair care, etc. Attractive people are more persuasive.

❑ Broadcast your credentials in a way that appears natural and not braggy. People admire talent but they hate bragging.

❑ Brand yourself as a winner. If people expect you to win, they will be biased toward making it happen.

❑ Meet in the most impressive space you can control. This creates a physical and visual impression that broadcasts your power, talent, and success.

❑ Set expectations ahead of time. If people expect you to ask for the moon, they will be delighted when you agree to accept less. And when people expect you to be the better negotiator, they will be subtly biased toward that outcome.

❑ Pre-suade with thoughts and images that will bias people toward a frame of mind that is compatible with your upcoming persuasion. For example, if you want someone to be generous with you, prime the pump with an unrelated story of kindness.

❑ Bring high energy. People with high energy are more persuasive. We're all drawn to energy.

This checklist will help you set the table for persuasion, but you still need a lot of technique once you are in the same room. Let's talk about technique next.

GO BIGLY OR GO HOME

Whenever there is mass confusion and complexity, people automatically gravitate to the strongest, most confident voice. We humans don't like uncertainty, so we are attracted to those who offer clarity and simple answers, even if the answers are wrong or incomplete. Master Persuaders can thrive in chaotic environments by offering the clarity people crave. And if an environment is not chaotic already, a skilled persuader who understands both social media and the news business can easily stir the pot to create an advantage through chaos. Candidate Trump was a champion of this method.

There is an old banking saying: If you borrow a million dollars from a bank, the bank essentially owns you. But if you borrow $10 billion, you own the bank. That's because the bank can foreclose on your measly million-dollar loan without much pain on its side, but the bank would have trouble surviving if it wrote off a $10 billion loss. The bank is forced to work with a large borrower, and maybe renegotiate terms. But the million-dollar borrower is out of luck because the bank has all the power at that dollar level.

This reminds me a lot of Trump's strategy of sucking all the energy out of the news cycle until his competition had no way to breathe. If Trump had tiptoed into the election, the mainstream media would have owned him. And they would have treated him like a clown, before moving on to talk about his competition. So Trump didn't tiptoe. He went in so hard, and so provocatively, that the media had no economic choice but to focus on him. He was pure gold for the press. And because of that, he came to own them, at least in the limited sense of dominating their news cycle.

If you don't know a lot about persuasion, or strategy, or the news media's business model, you might have seen Trump's actions as symptoms of narcissism and buffoonery, nothing more. You might have asked yourself who in their right mind would *intentionally* be so provocative as to attract nonstop negative news coverage. The answer is a Master Persuader. The extra criticism was worth the pain because it sucked up all the media attention and rendered his Republican primary challengers invisible.

Amazingly, Trump's strategy worked even though the news coverage it invited was overwhelmingly negative. This highlights a dividing line between a normal trained persuader and a true Master Persuader. Trump probably knew that one arrow in the chest could kill him, but if he had a thousand arrows, lined up just right, he could sleep on top of their pointy ends the same way a bed of nails works. No individual arrow's point has to support much weight if you bunch them closely together. Trump deactivated the incoming attacks by ensuring there were too many of them. The news business has to cover the newest stories, at the expense of the old ones. Trump could relegate any unflattering story to the back burner by introducing new provocations (often via tweet) every day.

How do I know Trump was cleverly and intentionally hogging all of the press attention—both good and bad—and not simply flailing around? We have reports that Trump told people in advance he planned to suck all the oxygen out of the race.[1] That doesn't mean it happened. But by the end of this book, I hope to persuade you it would be consistent with Trump's persuasion skills.

Trump used his mastery of the news cycle to create the impression that he was the most important person running for president, even if you hated him. When people are important, we start to feel they must be capable too, at least to some degree, because being capable is usually what makes people important. Our minds are primed to see important, capable people as leaders. And that instinct—to follow the most important and capable leader—can be more influential than facts and policies.

Trump was confident and clear about his priorities. But he was famously unclear about his preferred policy details. That is good persuasion technique. It allowed supporters to see whatever they wanted to see. But the details never mattered as much as the big picture. And the big picture was that Trump was a clear and strong voice in a scary and confusing world.

IS PRESIDENT TRUMP A "NATURAL" PERSUADER?

T he question I heard the most during the election of 2016 was about the source of Trump's persuasion talent. Was he a "natural," or did he learn his technique in some rigorous fashion? The question matters because if he learned his skills, you can learn them too. But if he is a natural, you might be out of luck. I don't know the full answer to the question, but I can tell you it looks more like technique than lucky genes to me. Almost everything Trump does is persuasion correct, based on best practices in the fields of business and persuasion, as far as I can tell. It would be hard to be so consistent without a deep knowledge of the tools of persuasion.

Let's look at the clues to see how much of Trump's persuasion is based on training and knowledge versus natural ability.

THE NORMAN VINCENT PEALE CONNECTION

In the 1970s, Fred and Mary Trump and their kids started attending Marble Collegiate Church in New York City, which had a famous pastor named Norman Vincent Peale.[1] Young readers of this book might not recognize that name, but people above a certain age know him as the author of the super successful book *The Power of Positive Thinking*. It was a mega-best seller. Peale is one of the most important authors and thinkers in American history. He influenced millions.

Including me.

Peale told me I could do anything if I simply *thought about it the right way*. It was a huge perceptual shift and it freed me from the prison I had created in my own mind. So I used my powers of positive thinking to focus on someday becoming a rich and famous cartoonist who can do his work while sitting by the beach.

I'm writing this paragraph at the beach.

True story.

Peale was good. He was very good.

Peale's book taught people about the power of the mind and its ability to author a great life. You can see in Trump a type of positive thinking that appears to be important to his success. The public has now watched more than once as Trump imagined succeeding in a new field and then did it. Evidently, he doesn't see any limit on how successful he can be. Trump has said in interviews that Peale was a big influence on him. It is hard to know how much, but you can see the Peale "filter" coming through in everything Trump does. In some sense, Trump *thought* himself into the presidency.

Oh, and one more interesting thing about Peale: In his day, people accused him of being a hypnotist.[2] Apparently he was so persuasive that some people assumed he had a secret skill set. I wouldn't call Peale's methods hypnosis, but he was a Master Persuader for sure. And Trump learned it from the source.

The best source ever.

So if Trump is a "natural," it would be quite a coincidence that he had so much contact with a Master Persuader of the highest caliber.

As an aside, I would love to see a study of the other kids who attended Peale's church. I'll bet the quality of their lives is above average. But that's just an educated guess.

THE ART OF THE DEAL

Trump authored one of the most popular books of all time on the topic of negotiating, which is a special form of persuasion. The book is *The Art of the Deal*, published in 1987.

His coauthor, Tony Schwartz, did the writing, but it shows Trump's interest in the topic of persuasion. You tend to learn the things that you care about. And Trump cares about negotiating. He mentions it nearly every day. And obviously he often negotiated over the course of his career.

Years ago I learned of something called reticular activation. In this context, it refers to the brain's natural ability to filter out information that you don't need, making it is easier to spot the things you do need. That's why you can hear someone call your name in a noisy room when you can't make out any other words. Your name is important to you, so your brain has a sensitive filter for it. In general, we notice things that matter and ignore things that don't. We have to do this because otherwise the environment would be sending too many signals to our little brains at the same time.

After 1987, when *The Art of the Deal* was a huge best seller, Trump's brain became "tuned" to the topics of negotiating and persuasion. He made negotiating his brand, and that means his brain started to recognize other persuasion methods in his environment because that was his new filter. Negotiating was important to Trump, so he was more likely to seek new information on the topic, casually and otherwise. In other words, even if you think Trump's coauthor wrote every word of *The Art of the Deal*, and even if you think Trump knew little about negotiating in 1987, the fact that it became his brand virtually guaranteed he would become an expert in it over time simply because his filters were set to absorb that kind of information. And the topic is easily absorbed. It isn't physics.

I had a similar experience after taking hypnosis classes. Once my filters were set to notice persuasion, I saw it everywhere. I was more likely to notice persuasion-related headlines and to read them. I was more likely to notice persuasion in life and to analyze those situations to understand the key variables. I became a persuasion-knowledge magnet. And I learned a lot about persuasion, over time, without really trying. Trump's situation was similar. Once he branded himself as a great negotiator, it almost guaranteed he would learn a lot more on the topic going forward.

It would be hard for a "natural" persuader to be pitch-perfect in persuasion. You might expect a natural but untrained persuader to exaggerate, play on your emotions, and use visual imagery. You would expect to see all the tricks of a car salesperson too. But all of those tricks are common knowledge, and they don't speak to any *deep* training in persuasion. A highly trained persuader would display more complexity in persuasion. It would look more engineered, if you knew what you were looking for.

The following chapters will lift the lid on Trump's persuasion so you can see the engineering. It is impressive.

PART 4

HOW TO USE PERSUASION IN BUSINESS AND POLITICS

HOW TO DESIGN A
LINGUISTIC KILL SHOT

O ver the course of the election we saw Trump assign one sticky nickname after another to his opponents. It seemed as if each new nickname was a winner. Clinton's team tried a few nicknames for Trump, but they failed. Badly. None of this is a coincidence. Trump's nicknames were deeply engineered and then tested in front of live audiences. Here are some of his winners.

- Low-energy Jeb
- Lyin' Ted
- Crooked Hillary
- Pocahontas
- Goofy Elizabeth Warren
- Cryin' Chuck Schumer (came later)

Compare Trump's success with the underwhelming branding efforts that came from the Clinton side:

- Donald Duck
- Dangerous Donald
- Drumpf

You don't have to be a trained persuader to see the difference in quality. But you probably don't recognize all the technique in Trump's nicknames. If you thought the names were nothing more than common insults, you missed a lot of his persuasion engineering. I'll walk you through it in this chapter.

How powerful were Trump's nicknames? So powerful that the day I heard Trump say "Low-energy Jeb" I predicted Bush was done, and blogged that opinion on August 27, 2015. Keep in mind that literally no other pundits saw this nickname as important to the election when they first heard it. But I could see its power because my brain has a filter to spot persuasion. In time, I saw a pattern emerge in Trump's naming choices:

Trump used words that were uncommon in political campaigns, to violate our expectations and make his branding memorable. Examples: "low-energy," "crooked," and "lyin'."

Trump's nicknames were *visually* compatible with the person he was branding. For example, Jeb Bush did appear to have low energy (after Trump biased us by telling us to look for it).

Trump's nicknames anticipated future confirmation bias to make them stickier and more powerful over time. We all knew "Lyin' Ted" Cruz would say things in the future that the fact-checkers would flag, because all politicians do. In time, even his accurate and honest statements would start to look suspicious, thanks to confirmation bias and Trump's sticky nickname.

Trump's nicknames were designed for strategic contrast. Many voters didn't trust Trump's honesty and motives, so he labeled his main primary opponent Lyin' Ted and his general election competitor Crooked Hillary. That reduced the contrast between his credibility and that of his competition.

Trump's nicknames were a form of the High-Ground Maneuver, in which you leave the details in the weeds and focus on bigger concepts where we all agree. You might have liked Hillary Clinton's proposed policies, but would you risk putting a "crooked" person in the Oval Office?

Let's look at how Trump's nicknames follow the formula.

LYIN' TED

Trump cleverly chose nicknames that were not the type of words you normally see in politics. The normal insults that politicians traditionally sling at one another are too overused and boring to be sticky. For example, labeling an opponent a "liberal" would just make you yawn.

Politicians often accuse one another of lying. But they are usually talking about a specific situation. It is far more unusual, and far more provocative, to label the *person* a liar. It would be considered undiplomatic behavior. And that minor bit of wrongness helps the method work. It is just slightly more provocative than you expect from a politician. That draws your attention and makes you remember it.

But Trump apparently wanted to squeeze some extra juice from the word "lying" and make his branding stand out. So he insisted that *Lyin'* Ted was the proper spelling, not *Lying* Ted. This was good branding. It was different from anything you have seen in politics and it gave you a reason to pause and wonder why it mattered if the spelling was "lyin'" or "lying." It did matter, but only because you stopped and wondered about it. That is an engineered mental pause for persuasion. Trump wants you to stop and think about his choice of "lyin'" over "lying." The fact that you spent time thinking about it helps you remember the name. It also uses a trick called "making you think past the sale." In this case the sale is the idea that Ted Cruz lies. You end up accidentally accepting that idea because you spent time thinking about the best way to write "lyin'." That's strong persuasion engineering.

The Lyin' Ted label had another big persuasion element that most people missed. You would have to be a trained persuader to even notice. Trump engineers his nicknames for future confirmation bias. By that I mean he primed our brains to see the future through his filter. Anytime Ted Cruz said anything we deemed untrue, we immediately thought of the nickname and it reinforced the association. And our minds irrationally assign importance to whatever we think about the most.

What were the odds that Cruz would say things during the campaign that you thought were untrue? 100 percent. He was a politician in a political race. They all say untrue things, or so we think. It was a perfect future trap. Lyin' Ted was destined to do more lyin' just by existing and being a candidate. Confirmation bias would help us see more lyin' than was actually there.

And there's the visual element: Ted Cruz has an unfortunate beady-eyed-liar look. If you were a movie director, you would cast him as the bad guy. He just doesn't look honest.

Here I pause to say I know nothing of Ted Cruz's record of honesty. I have no idea whether he is better or worse than any other politician. I'm focusing on his physical appearance and Trump's persuasion. And on those levels, Lyin' Ted simply *looked* like a liar. The reality might be very different, but that doesn't matter to our story today. What matters is that the Lyin' Ted nickname stuck like glue. It was fresh political wording, it was provocative, it had a visual element in Cruz's liar-looking face, and it was designed to get stronger over time with confirmation bias.

You can't engineer persuasion better than that.

LIL' MARCO

During the Republican primary season Trump nicknamed Senator Marco Rubio "Lil' Marco." This too was superb persuasion engineering. Almost nothing in life that is good is also "little." It's a negative word all by itself, and it can apply to anything from Rubio's personality to his potential to his plans for the country to his physical height. Rubio isn't short by normal standards, but he is shorter than Trump, and that's all that mattered. Anytime you saw them standing together you were reminded of the nickname.

Once again we see the persuader's engineering.

"Little" is not a typical insult in politics. It is fresh. But Trump freshens it further by making it "Lil'."

Rubio's physical appearance matched the label. He is somewhat baby faced and young for a politician.

The nickname created a confirmation bias: Every time you saw Rubio stand next to a taller human it made you think of his smallness. Historically, the taller candidate usually wins the presidency. Humans are biased to interpret physical size as a leadership quality. That instinct is probably left over from cave-dwelling days.

And we see "little" as a negative word on its own.

CROOKED HILLARY

Now that you know the formula, let's speed through the Crooked Hillary nickname.

"Crooked" is a fresh word for a political insult. Check!

Clinton's health was a campaign question (thanks to me, in part). She needed help getting up and down stairs, and she once collapsed getting into her car. It was easy to imagine her posture as "crooked," and that gives you the visual persuasion. Check!

Again there was a confirmation bias: Trump knew that there would be lots of opportunities to remind voters that Clinton was up to something "crooked." The Clinton Foundation and her hacked e-mail server provided plenty of fodder. Once Trump primed you to see Clinton as crooked, it was easy to see everything she did as fitting that description, even when it didn't. That's how confirmation bias works. Check!

And as I already mentioned, the "crooked" label is a High-Ground Maneuver compared to the details of her policy ideas. Voters can disagree on policy, but we all agree that a crooked president is a bad idea. Check!

POCAHONTAS AND GOOFY
ELIZABETH WARREN

One of Trump's leading critics on the left was Senator Elizabeth Warren. You have to know some backstory on Warren to know why Trump picked "Pocahontas" as one of her nicknames. Warren had at one time in the past claimed to have Native American blood. It turns out she can't substantiate that claim. Apparently her family believed they had Native American ancestors, so it wasn't a lie. She was just wrong. And her wrongness on that question became the most famous story about her. Trump made it more famous by calling her Pocahontas whenever she criticized him publicly.

In this case, there was no opportunity for engineering any future confirmation bias into the nickname because it was a story from the past. It was yesterday's news. But the public didn't know much else about Warren, so Trump didn't have much fodder to work with.

Trump chose "Pocahontas" for several reasons that I think you can start to recognize by now. It was visual, in the sense that you imagine her in full Native American garb when you hear it. It makes you stop and think. And if you don't understand the reference, it might make you search online to find out what it means. That's good too, because it makes you remember it. "Pocahontas" is—once again—a fresh insult for politics. And it reminded voters that Warren had some alleged truth problems in the past.

But best of all, it was silly. And it was easy to meme. The Internet loved it. The silliness of it detracted from Warren's credibility and gravitas. We heard her talking, but in our minds she was doing a Native American war dance in face paint and feathered headgear. It was harder to take her seriously after the nickname did its damage. Trump also referred to Warren as "goofy," which works along the same lines to minimize her credibility.

And while you can disagree with the details of Warren's criticisms of Trump, we all agree that goofy people are not our role models. And we don't need to take them seriously.

CLINTON'S NICKNAME FAILURES

If you still think Trump didn't use deep persuasion engineering in his nicknames, compare them with Clinton's attempts, including those from her supporters. They are completely empty of persuasion. Or worse.

First we saw the Internet trying to turn Trump's Americanized name back to its Austrian root: Drumpf. The name is unusual, which is good persuasion, but I can't see anything else it has going for it. Still, the word became viral because it sounded vaguely insulting. But it wasn't persuasive.

Trump's critics literally avoided saying his name early in the process because they didn't want to show respect or give attention to such a monster. And perhaps they didn't want to use Trump's name because "trump" is synonymous with victory. But assigning a foreign-sounding name to Trump, and implying that the name was an insult, was incompatible with Clinton's pro-immigration platform. And the mainstream media never picked up on the Drumpf nickname because Clinton herself didn't use it. By election day, the name had mostly disappeared from social media.

A hidden-camera video by Project Veritas revealed that some of Clinton's operatives were pushing the idea of calling Trump "Donald Duck." The idea was to reinforce the idea that Trump was "ducking" (avoiding) showing his tax returns and whatever else he might want to avoid in the future. Knowing that politicians like to avoid unfavorable topics, this nickname had the potential for future confirmation bias. That part was good. The problem here is that Donald Duck is a cute and beloved character associated with a respected brand. And the Clinton persuasion messaging was focusing on Trump being a scary Hitler-in-waiting. Comparing him to a lovable duck is literally the opposite of what they needed. The nickname never went public. Someone was smart enough to stop it.

On top of the nickname's persuasion problems, "Donald Duck" is owned by ABC/Disney. There was no way their lawyers would let Clinton's team associate the character with Trump, who was by then being compared to Hitler. Every part of that nickname plan was bad.

Some Clinton supporters floated the idea of giving Trump the nickname "Dangerous Donald."[1] The name had some advantages. It fit the

Clinton campaign's main persuasion theme that said Trump was too dangerous to have his finger on the nuclear button. It was a good future-confirmation-bias trap, as Trump was likely to do or say dangerous-sounding things. And "dangerous" is a fresh word in politics. That's all good.

The problem is that Trump supporters wanted a dangerous candidate. It wasn't going to change their minds about anything. And dangerous might be just the thing you needed to "drain the swamp" in Washington DC, as Trump famously said, defeat ISIS, and secure the borders. "Dangerous" was too easy to flip to a positive.

Notice that Trump's nicknames have no flipping potential. There is no political context in which being low energy, little, lying, or crooked is a good thing. But you can think of plenty of times that a dangerous person has been the right fit for a dangerous job. The military comes to mind. And Harry Truman was dangerous, dropping two nuclear bombs on Japan. Even President Obama was dangerous when he took out Bin Laden in Pakistan.

By election day, Trump still had no sticky nicknames from the Left. They tried, but their technique was lacking.

HOW TO USE VISUAL PERSUASION

Humans are visual creatures. We believe our eyes before we believe whatever faulty opinions are coming from our other senses. So if you want to persuade, use visual language and visual imagery. The difference in effectiveness is enormous.

People often asked me during the election if I was being too generous about Trump's persuasion talents. The more popular opinion of Trump at the time, and perhaps when you read this book as well, was that his so-called persuasion was little more than lying about everything that mattered. It doesn't take much talent to lie. But people who are not trained in persuasion would miss the technique. And most of all, they would miss the consistency of it. It would be one thing if Trump used some persuasion tricks now and then. It is a different matter when you see persuasion applied consistently and with the strongest known tools. That can be interpreted as accidental only for so long. When you see the consistency of Trump's visual persuasion—one of his many techniques—it is hard to write it off as coincidence. You'll need some examples, so here they are.

PERSUASION TIP 19

In the context of
persuasion, you don't
need a physical picture if
you can make someone
imagine the scene.

THE WALL

Trump could have simply said he wanted better immigration control, but that would not have been good visual persuasion. Concepts without images are weak sauce. So instead, Trump sold us a mental image of a "big, beautiful wall." He said "wall" so many times that we all started to picture it. Before long, we started seeing artists' renderings of potential walls. Even the opposition media started running videos of existing walls and walls in other countries.

The reason the wall imagery was good persuasion is that it was both simple to understand and memorable, compared with a generic concept such as "border control." And it made us "think past the sale." In other words, we reflexively assumed the wall would exist because we had imagined it so often and debated its cost. That's one of a persuader's most basic and well-known tricks: People automatically gravitate toward the future they are imagining most vividly, even if they don't want the future they are seeing. You've probably experienced something similar in your own life. When you vividly imagine something you *don't* want to happen, such as dropping your phone in the toilet, it can (for some people) increase the odds it will happen. Humans are visual creatures. Like moths, we are drawn to the brightest light. And the brightest light in our minds is whatever we can visualize most clearly. This sort of persuasion doesn't work on every person in every situation. It isn't *that* powerful. But in the context of a yearlong presidential campaign, in which you only need to persuade perhaps 5 percent of the public in order to win, every advantage counts. Trump took every persuasion advantage available, especially the ones that were free. His opponents did not.

While Trump was talking about the wall, Senator Rand Paul—one of Trump's Republican primary challengers—had a number of smart ideas that got no traction whatsoever. Paul presented his ideas as concepts without visuals. They died on arrival.

Trump was also smart enough to be vague about the details of the wall so that each of us could imagine the wall we wanted to imagine. He could have easily provided his own artists' renderings of the wall, but that would have been a mistake. It would have given critics lots of targets to attack. But there is one kind of wall that is hard to criticize: the one that is entirely different in each person's head.

In my imagination, I started seeing small segments of the wall as attractive tourist destinations and special trade zones, with lots of potential for mutual benefit on both sides. Others probably imagined a harsh wall that said, "Stay out!" because that's what they wanted or expected to see.

Trump's critics often mentioned the impracticality of building a solid wall along the entire border. They said it would be cost prohibitive. And walls work well only in certain types of terrain. Trump acknowledged that reality a few times, but he generally stuck with his oversimplification of "the wall" because it is easy to visualize, easy to chant, and easy to remember. Compare . . .

Bad persuasion: We will use a variety of means to improve border security.

Good persuasion: We will build a big, beautiful wall.

The bad persuasion with no visuals is the more honest and accurate of the two. The good-persuasion example simplifies to the point of being inaccurate. Only one of those approaches moves the ball forward, and it isn't the one that is accurate. Trump chose the less accurate approach with a bias for action. You will see that same bias in much of what he does, and almost always at the expense of the details that won't make much difference to us in the long run.

When persuasion is simplified to the point of being inaccurate, do the ends justify the means? It depends what you think about the alternatives.

ISIS AND THOSE CAGES

When Trump talked about ISIS, he always did it with scary visual imagery. He said ISIS "chops off heads" and "drowns people in cages." You can't get any scarier, or more visual, than that. And that persuasion gave him space to be the biggest badass on the topic, to the point of frightening half of America in the process. That positioning served him well for getting elected. If you were a voter who feared terror attacks, Trump made a persuasive case for being the toughest commander in chief. Visual imagery was vital for that framing.

ISIS IN THE VATICAN

Here's a brilliant example of visual persuasion, as I described it in my blog.

Posted August 20, 2015

When CNN anchor Chris Cuomo asked Trump to react to the Pope's criticism of capitalism, Trump correctly saw it as a trap. The way the question was posed, he could either agree with the Pope, thereby criticizing capitalism, which would have been weird, or he could say the Pope was wrong, which would be risky. Both moves would be losers.

Trump couldn't bluntly refuse to engage in the question because that would look weak. So how does Trump wiggle out of such a well-crafted media trap?

Trump responds that he would tell the Pope that ISIS is coming to get him, and that they have plans to take over the Vatican, which I assume is true, or true enough.

Do you even remember the question anymore?

Now compare the wattage coming from these two thoughts:

1. A boring discussion about corruption in capitalism (Cuomo's question)

2. A mental picture of ISIS taking over the Vatican

No comparison. Corruption and capitalism are mere concepts that have no visual appeal. The ideas are important yet inert. But an ISIS overthrow of the Vatican is so visual that you wonder why it isn't already a movie. And that visual is all anyone will remember of that interview in a week.

ROSIE O'DONNELL

I mentioned earlier in the book that Trump referred to Rosie O'Donnell in the first Republican debate as his strategy to dodge a question about his past comments about women. That was visual persuasion because we immediately see her in our minds. I include it again here for completeness, so you can see how consistent Trump is with visual persuasion.

BEN CARSON'S BELT BUCKLE

During the Republican primaries, Dr. Ben Carson briefly challenged Trump for the lead in the polls. Trump took him out of the contest by using visual persuasion. You might remember Trump acting out the alleged belt-buckle stabbing that Carson mentioned in his book. Trump stepped away from the podium at his campaign rally and mimed the attack while mocking it at the same time. Every media outlet carried his acting job. It was deeply visual and disturbing. Carson's numbers dropped at about the same time, and never recovered. I publicly predicted Carson's demise the day I saw Trump's performance about the belt buckle.

TRUMP PROPERTIES

Trump had a natural visual advantage for his accomplishments in the form of Trump properties (hotels, golf courses, etc.) around the world. Every time you saw one of those hotels you were reminded of his success. Compare that with the Clinton Foundation's accomplishments, which had no visual element.

AMERICA THE VISUAL

Trump always paid attention to the colors and symbols associated with his brand as a candidate. Consider...

You never saw him dress casually during the campaign. To do so would have removed some gravitas.

His shirt was always white, and his tie colors were always in the color palette of the American flag. None of this is coincidence.

As I'll describe in more detail in the next chapter, Trump agreed to appear on *Saturday Night Live* on a set designed to look like the Oval Office, flags and all. The candidates appearing on *SNL* would have had veto rights over any skit concepts. That means he agreed to appear in the one with the best imagery. That isn't an accident.

Trump's private jet reminds you of Air Force One. Your brain can't help but make that connection. If social media is our guide, a lot of people noticed the similarity in aircraft. Trump owned the jet long before he became a candidate for president, but you can bet he planned his flight schedule for maximum impact. The media fed us images of Clinton exiting her high-end jet that didn't look at all like Air Force One, while we saw Trump walking down the runway from his Boeing 757 looking as if he were already president.

When you think of Hillary Clinton, how many iconic symbols of America spring to mind? For most of you, the answer will be none.

HOW TO MAKE PEOPLE
IMAGINE YOU AS PRESIDENT

From the day that Trump announced his candidacy, his biggest persuasion challenge was that people literally couldn't *imagine* him as president. We can easily imagine boring old senators and governors becoming presidents. But it was tough to imagine this orange ball of provocation sitting in the Oval Office. And so I watched in awe as Trump methodically fixed his biggest problem by helping us *imagine* his presidency until we could do it on our own. His best persuasion move on this front involved his appearance on the late-night television show *Saturday Night Live*.

I have enough experience appearing on TV and radio—having done it several hundred times—that I know some things that the general public wouldn't necessarily know. One thing I know is that a guest as important as a presidential candidate gets a hard veto over any skit they are in. And that means Trump approved the *SNL* skit that imagined him as president and working in the Oval Office. I have a distinct memory of Trump in the Oval Office on *SNL*, but I can't remember a single joke from the skit. Visual memory overwhelms any other kind of memory, and vision is the most persuasive of your senses.

I assume the jokes on *SNL* that night were at Trump's expense. I assume the humor was edgy but not so bad that Trump would veto any of it. *SNL* allowed Trump to show his sense of humor, which is one of his strengths. But more important, it created a future "visual memory" of Trump in the Oval Office. If you saw that episode live, or on social media later, you suddenly had an easy way to imagine Trump as president. *SNL* did that for him.

Compare Trump's skit with Hillary Clinton's appearance on *Saturday Night Live*. She approved a skit in which she played a bartender named Val who was serving a drunken Hillary Clinton who was played by one of the *SNL* cast. The visual we got from that was that Clinton loves alcohol— maybe too much. That is just about the worst image you could present for a presidential candidate. And it is doubly bad because of the *power of contrast*. Trump was a rare nondrinking candidate for president. He was competing for a job that required sobriety at all hours of the day. And thanks to *SNL*, he was competing against the image of a drunk.

After seeing how both candidates handled their *SNL* choices, my opinion of Trump's chances was set in concrete. Barring any surprises (and there were plenty to come), this was not going to be a fair fight. To me it looked like a massacre in the making.

In political terms, and looking back at the *SNL* skit, if you are helping people think of you as the president of the United States while your competitor is self-branding as a barfly, you are right where you want to be.

Here are a few comics on the power of contrast.

Within a few days of President Trump's inauguration, he had signed a flurry of executive orders, stirred up several controversies, and created more news per hour than anyone had imagined possible. I blogged at the time that it was brilliant persuasion. I wrote a post on it and titled it "Dilution Outrage."

Posted January 26, 2017

I'm having a fun time watching President Trump flood the news cycle with so many stories and outrages that no one can keep up. Here's how the math of persuasion works in this situation:

1 outrage out of 3 headlines in a week: bad persuasion

25 outrages out of 25 headlines in a week: excellent persuasion

At the moment, there are so many outrages, executive orders, protests, and controversies that none of them can get enough oxygen in our brains. I can't obsess about problem X because the rest of the alphabet is coming at me at the same time.

When you encounter a situation that is working great except for one identifiable problem, you can focus on the problem and try to fix it. But if you have a dozen complaints at the same time, none of them looks special. The whole situation just looks confusing, and you don't know where to start. So you wait and see what happens. Humans need contrast in order to make solid decisions that turn into action. Trump removed all of your contrast by providing multiple outrages of similar energy.

You're probably seeing the best persuasion you will ever see from a new president. Instead of dribbling out one headline at a time, so the vultures and critics can focus their fire, Trump has flooded the playing field. You don't know where to aim your outrage. He's creating so many opportunities for disagreement that it's mentally exhausting. Literally. He's wearing down the critics, replacing their specific complaints with entire encyclopedias of complaints. And when Trump has created a hundred reasons to complain, do you know what impression will be left with the public?

He sure got a lot done.

Even if you don't like it.

In only a few days, Trump has made us question what the hell every other president was doing during their first weeks in office. Were they even trying?

Update: Trump's strong start got bogged down by Congress, and the courts, soon after I wrote this section. His most notable early "failure" was the first version of an Obamacare replacement. And you know why it failed?

Because the contrast with Obamacare wasn't good.

Every decision is a comparison of alternatives. If you control how people see the alternatives, you can sell anything. Trump did a great job of eroding the credibility of Obamacare, but the first GOP plan for its replacement failed on the contrast level because experts said fewer people would be covered.

The best persuasion play for health care would be to create a bill that covers *more* people, one way or another. That is a winning contrast. Covering fewer people is a losing contrast. The other details of the bill hardly matter when you have that problem.

I am writing this before the next health-care bill is crafted. My prediction is that if the new one covers fewer people, it will likely fail. If it covers more people, it will probably pass.

You can use the power of contrast to improve every part of your professional and personal life. Here are some suggestions to get you started.

Participate in activities at which you excel compared with others. People's impression of you as talented and capable compared with the average participant will spill over to the rest of your personal brand.

In business, always present your ideas in the context of alternatives that are clearly worse. Don't just sell your proposed solution; slime all the other options with badness.

If someone you know is treating a small issue as a big one, remind them what a big problem looks like. That can reframe how they process their small worries.

Always remember that people make decisions in the context of alternatives. If you aren't framing the alternatives as bad, you are not persuading at all.

HOW I GOT THE VP
PREDICTION WRONG

Here's a story that highlights the power of contrast. Notice how often I circle back to this theme. Contrast is essential to persuasion.

My critics like to point out that I made a few wrong predictions about Trump's pick for his VP running mate. In those failings you can see the limits of persuasion as a predictor. The VP decision involved lots of variables that are invisible to the public. We don't know how the candidates get along personally. We don't know what kind of scandals the background checks turned up. We don't know how interested any particular candidate would be in taking the job. Persuasion is not a predictive variable in those cases. But in the spirit of evaluating the Persuasion Filter, I confess that I publicly suggested in February of 2016 that Mark Cuban would be a powerful VP pick for Trump to make the ticket seem less scary to Democrats. I stopped short of predicting that Trump would choose Cuban, but it was close enough to a prediction that I'll acknowledge I missed it anyway. As it turned out, Cuban became one of Trump's leading critics. That's as big a miss as you can get. I will, however, take credit for writing in that same blog post that Cuban would be a good pick because he would be willing to turn on Trump the minute it looked like the right thing to do. And turn he did, when he thought it was the right thing to do (I assume), endorsing Clinton and becoming one of the loudest of the Trump critics.

Later, in February of 2016, I predicted that Chris Christie would be a good pick for the VP job. Christie got along with Trump, was early to endorse him, and is a fighter, like Trump. But I didn't stick with that prediction.

By May 2016, I had updated my VP prediction to say ex-Senator Scott Brown would be the best fit. He was an experienced politician, and handsome—which matters even if you think it shouldn't. As written, I wasn't *exactly* making a prediction, but I'll call it a prediction anyway to make my bigger point when I get to it.

Now compare my accurate predictions throughout the campaign with my misses on the VP selection. The pattern tells you a lot about the dynamics of persuasion. It is hard to predict what *one* person will do with *one* decision at *one* specific time. But it is relatively easy to predict that a Master Persuader with twenty-four-hour news coverage and a massive social media following, operating for over a year, could sway enough voters to win in a country that is normally about evenly split.

Time is always on the side of the persuader. If you give me enough time, and I repeat the same message often enough, I can sway 5 percent of any crowd to believe anything. And 5 percent is usually enough to win the presidency in the United States because most elections are close affairs due to party loyalties.

I had never heard of Mike Pence before Trump selected him as his VP running mate. But as soon as I saw Pence, and heard him speak, I knew he was a strong pick from a persuasion perspective. And that's because of the *power of contrast*.

On a strategic and political level, Pence was a smart pick because he consolidated the Republican conservative base. And Trump had said he wanted a seasoned politician, which the public and pundits agreed was a good idea. Pence had experience as both a governor and a senator, which is about as good as you can get. So on all the dimensions that people normally value for a VP pick, Pence checked the boxes. He even won his only debate against Clinton's VP running mate, Tim Kaine.

But that isn't the whole story. The real story is about the *power of contrast*.

The last thing a presidential candidate wants is for pundits and voters to start wondering why the number two person isn't the number one person. You need a VP running mate whom the country takes seriously, but one who also has far less charisma than the top of the ticket. Pence created a perfect contrast to Trump. Not only did he add the seriousness that voters wanted, but when he stood next to Trump, he literally looked like the washed-out version. Pence is like a black-and-white photograph compared with Trump's multimedia looks and personality. Pence is one of the most experienced and capable politicians our country has ever produced, but he still disappears in Trump's charisma field. That's perfect persuasion because voters respond to contrast more than they do to facts and reason.

The best example of the contrast principle was Ronald Reagan picking George H. W. Bush as his running mate. Bush was a deeply experienced politician, but boring compared with Reagan's star power. Reagan went on to become such a popular president that Bush was the automatic front-runner for the job after Reagan served two terms. But Bush had a contrast problem of his own. He needed to pick a running mate who looked substantial enough to be taken seriously while still creating a favorable contrast for Bush. That didn't give him much room to operate.

Bush was boring compared with Reagan, but now Bush needed his own running mate who could make Bush-the-boring look like a natural leader by contrast. Enter Dan Quayle. He was weaker than Bush, who was weaker than Reagan. That's a lot of dilution. And it is no surprise that Quayle did not go on to the presidency. He didn't even stay on the ticket when Bush ran for reelection. Quayle was two levels of charisma away from Reagan.

Mike Pence might someday have the same contrast problem. If Trump has a successful presidency, Pence has a good chance of being the next Republican candidate for president. That means Pence would need to choose for his running mate a more boring version of himself. And that future VP candidate would be two levels of charisma away from Trump. That's too much of a gap.

PERSUASION TIP 20

People are more persuaded by contrast than by facts or reason. Choose your contrasts wisely.

Had I known Mike Pence was a potential VP pick, I think I would have ranked him in the top three options without knowing much about him except his looks, his job experience, and his Republican credentials.

HOW TO PERSUADE
BY ASSOCIATION

One of the easiest forms of persuasion involves associating one image or idea with another in a way that makes some of the goodness (or badness) of one rub off on the other. That's the idea behind celebrity endorsements, labeling political opponents Nazis, and marketing in general. But you already knew that.

What you might not know is that each of us is "marketing" all the time. If you want to be liked and respected, you have to watch your accidental associations. For example, I know people who think bathroom humor is hilarious. I'm not here to judge their sense of humor, as that is subjective. The problem is that these folks think that sharing this sort of humor is nothing more than a laugh. But it is a *lot* more. It is persuasion by association. And if you tell enough bathroom jokes, your friends and family will literally start subconsciously associating you with shit. They might not be aware of the accidental persuasion. The way it manifests is that suddenly your friends feel too busy to get together with you.

The same concept holds for folks who talk endlessly about their own health problems. I care about people, and I want to know the gist of their situations. But if they dwell on it, and include visual descriptions and lots of details about their suffering, I start to see the person and the health problem as one and the same.

No one wants that.

When I was younger, I made all of the mistakes of association that I'm mentioning, and more. I figured that if something was funny, or appalling, it needed to be shared, all in the spirit of fun. My more experienced self tries to stick to topics that are interesting, useful, and positive. I still like jokes, obviously, but not the gross kind that lack cleverness.

As a general rule, I try to fill my brain with optimistic thoughts in order to crowd out the bad ones that sometimes slip in. This is a form of self-hypnosis, using the power of association. The positive thoughts lift my energy, which in turn lifts my mood, and even my immune system.

If you are trying to get past a negative thought or memory, try distracting yourself with positive images and ideas. Or change your scenery to something that has a positive vibe. You can program yourself all the way from a funk to a good mood if you change the inputs. And best of all, you can do the same to others. Fill their heads with positive thoughts and they will associate those good feelings with you. They couldn't separate those feelings if they tried.

If you want to make a good first impression, don't jokingly complain about the traffic on the way over. Try to work into the initial conversation some positive thoughts and images. Any positivity works. If your positivity has some visual imagery, that is even better. As the old saying goes, people won't always remember what you said, but they almost always remember how you made them feel.

You've probably heard it said that walking a dog is a great way to meet people. That's partly because dogs have such a powerful association with happiness, at least for dog lovers. If you love dogs, it is hard to be unhappy when you meet a new one. All of the good feelings you have had from every past dog transfer automatically to the new dog and its owner.

Another easy way to influence yourself by association is to decorate your living space in a way that you find emotionally pleasing. You can train yourself to enjoy a room so much that you become happy just by walking into it. Don't make the mistake of thinking that because your favorite color is gunmetal gray, it makes a good wall color. Ideally, you want wall colors that give you the right kind of energy for whatever you do in that room. Gray isn't usually the right answer.

As I'll describe in the next chapter, Trump got the advantage of persuasion by association when he crafted his campaign slogan to match

Ronald Reagan's. The persuasion works even if all it does is make the haters argue that you are *not* like Reagan at all. What matters is the mental association, not the details. And associating your name with Reagan is a good way to win the Republican nomination.

PERSUASION TIP 21

When you associate any two ideas or images, people's emotional reaction to them will start to merge over time.

HOW TO CREATE
EFFECTIVE CAMPAIGN
SLOGANS AND LOGOS

f you are just becoming acquainted with the concepts of cognitive dissonance and confirmation bias because of this book, you probably have no reliable way of sorting out Trump's "natural" persuasion instincts from his acquired knowledge. But I think the story becomes more clear when you look at Trump's campaign slogans and visual imagery compared with the losing effort on the Clinton side. I think all observers would agree that Trump won the branding battle. Bigly. Let's take a look at the technique he used to do it.

Trump's famous campaign slogan "Make America Great Again" was borrowed from Ronald Reagan's 1980 campaign, although Trump says he wasn't aware of it when he decided to use it.

And what happened when the media figured out that Trump was borrowing from Reagan? They wrote about it. They talked about it. They tried to turn it into a criticism about unoriginality without saying that directly. And when they were done with all that chatter, you remembered one thing: Ronald Reagan and Donald Trump have a similar vision.

That is a huge persuasion win, and it might have been an accident. Trump's biggest problem at the start was that he wasn't a career politician, and it was hard for the public to see him as one. The best persuasion solution in that situation is to graft your reputation to an outsider who not only became president but also became a legend in the job. Although Reagan had political experience as governor of California before becoming president, the public still has a reflex to think of him as an actor who became president, because that's the more interesting story. Reagan's success was the perfect pattern to put in people's heads. The pattern reminded us that an outsider *can* become one of the most beloved presidents in American history. Trump got all of that benefit by association from the start, and it never faded. That association alone would have made Trump's choice of slogans one of the best branding decisions of our lifetime, although as I said, it might have been an accident. But it goes deeper.

Now let's look at the words in "Make America Great Again." This is deep engineering. You won't see it clearly until we talk about Clinton's competing slogans and how bad they were. Your first impression in this chapter might be that I'm trying too hard to force a smart interpretation on Trump's choice of slogans. But wait until you see the full picture. For trained persuaders such as me, this is amazing.

Every word in "Make America Great Again" is active and powerful. Check it out:

Make: A power/dominance word that speaks of creation and manufacturing (i.e., jobs).

America: The strongest brand in every American voter's mind. It speaks to our identity and it fit comfortably with Trump's nationalist (America first) proposition.

Great: The word speaks to power/dominance and success.

Again: This word caused critics to debate whether America was already great or not. That's a nonsense debate because there is no agreed standard by which national greatness can be measured. But that doesn't matter for persuasion. What mattered is that the country was talking about Trump's slogan: Was it a mistake for Trump to include the word "again"? Did Reagan use that same word? Is the country really so bad now?

When you consider the Reagan association, the perfect fit with Trump's nationalist message, and the power in each word, you start to see the deep persuasion that is engineered into the slogan.

But Trump wasn't done yet.

He put the phrase on a red hat. Red is the boss of all colors. It is also the color associated with Republicans, which was convenient. But trust me when I say that if the Republican color had been a shade of baby blue, Trump would not have used that color in his brand. Any businessperson who understands branding knows the power of color. Red means action, dominance, and sex.[1] It was the perfect color for the Trump campaign. Compare that with the pink hats that became popular with Clinton supporters. Pink is the most wrong choice you can make if you are trying to persuade American men to join your team. Many women reject the color too. You can't do a worse job of color picking than that.

Trump's "Make America Great Again" slogan also did a perfect job of framing the situation as one in which individual citizens and their leaders focus on the betterment of America. You might think it is obvious that any campaign slogan should have that message. But compare that with one of Clinton's several failed campaign slogans: "I'm with her." That slogan doesn't speak to the betterment of the country. It literally suggests that citizens should be doing something for *one person*—Hillary Clinton. A campaign slogan can't fail much harder than that.

The slogan "Make America Great Again" was also catchy as all getout. It even has what I call in authors' lingo a *percussion* rhythm to it. A great sentence *sounds* good—in a way that music sounds good—independent of the meaning. The letters *M*, *K*, *G*, and *T* are powerful, like a drumbeat. Compare the powerful beat of **Make America Great Again** with the weak-sounding background hum of "I'm with Her." Not even close.

Trump's powerful slogan was born whole, and it rented a room in our brains on day one. It never left. It just got more powerful over time. But Clinton's team struggled and never found its brand. Among her poorly engineered slogans we saw:

- I'm with Her
- I'm Ready for Hillary
- Fighting for Us

- Breaking Down Barriers
- Stronger Together

The *New York Times* reported that the campaign cycled through eighty-five different slogan concepts before settling on "Stronger Together."[2] That sounds like committee work, and I doubt most of the participants had persuasion training. Trump allegedly came up with his slogan on his own.

Most of Clinton's slogans failed on the most basic level because they talked about the candidate and the party more than the country. In the context of the campaign, it seemed as if the unity those slogans represented was the unity of Clinton supporters themselves, not the country as a whole. Let's look at a few of Clinton's slogans individually.

"I'm with Her": This slogan emphasized Clinton's gender, implying that it must be some kind of advantage. As a man, I found this off-putting and tone deaf. It was also off message for someone running to be president of *all* Americans. My opinion doesn't represent men in general, but you only have to offend 5 percent of either gender to have a big problem. This slogan was more problem than solution.

"I'm Ready for Hillary": This slogan is about the voter, not the candidate, and certainly not the country. Worse yet, it assumes some sort of smug superiority in being "ready" for a woman president. There are no power words in the sentence and it is not the least bit catchy—which was a blessing in disguise in this case. This one didn't last long.

"Fighting for Us": Who is *us*? If Clinton intended "us" to mean Americans, why not say so? The implication is that the "us" is Clinton's supporters. Or maybe it refers to anyone who faces discrimination, such as women and minorities of all types. But whatever it was supposed to mean, it didn't sound like it was talking about America as a whole. For example, would a white male voter—a member of the patriarchy, in some people's opinion—think the slogan meant that Clinton would be fighting *for* him or *against* him?

"Breaking Down Barriers": This slogan suggests that Clinton's focus would be on fighting for the disadvantaged. But no matter how worthy that goal might be, in order to win the election, she had to get the support of voters who see the world in terms of winners and losers. Would those people breaking down barriers be taking jobs from the people on the other side? This slogan doesn't make anyone think of a win-win situation. It does have a good percussion to it. But that's all it has.

"**Stronger Together**": This slogan was the best of the bunch, and it got the most attention during the campaign. But while it seemed on the surface to be a harmless slogan about strength in numbers, things started to turn when Clinton's supporters became bullies, both online and in real life. Suddenly the "stronger together" theme started to sound like a pack of bullies attacking people who disagreed. Those bullies were indeed stronger together.

Yes, I know Trump supporters did bad things too. But their behavior didn't have a campaign slogan that made it sound more ominous than it already was. The "Stronger Together" slogan started to feel—at least to my ears—like an angry mob of bullies who didn't like the other half of the country.

THE MOLE

Hillary Clinton's persuasion game was so weak and backward on Twitter that I came up with the fun idea that her Twitter assistant must be a mole (a traitor) from the Trump campaign. The wrongness of Clinton's persuasion attempts on Twitter was so consistent that even today I wonder if it was intentional sabotage. My Twitter followers and I enjoyed spotting the alleged work of the Mole and tweeting about it. It was more fun than serious.

I was blogging and tweeting about "the Mole" for months, offering plenty of examples. I assumed that some of my writing on the topic was reaching the right people in the Clinton campaign. After all, much of the mainstream media was reading my blog. I know that because so many of them interviewed me or contacted me privately about what I wrote. So why didn't Clinton's social media people fix their easy-to-fix problem? That's still a mystery to me. Maybe the right person on Clinton's team never saw my criticisms. Or maybe the Mole was real. I doubt I will ever know.

The biggest recurring problem with Clinton's tweets was that she repeatedly asked voters to "Imagine President Trump" doing one thing or another that they thought would be bad. In the second dimension, that approach makes perfect sense. No one wants a president who is likely to do bad things. And making you imagine those bad things is normally a good persuasion tactic. That follows a trial lawyer approach of painting a picture and inviting the jury (in this case voters) to imagine being in the scene. Usually this is a solid persuasion technique. But it wasn't in this special case.

Here's why.

If you make voters *imagine* a President Trump, that makes it far easier for them to . . . wait for it . . . *imagine* a President Trump. And making voters imagine Trump as president was exactly what Trump was trying to do. This worked perfectly to help solve his biggest problem—voters couldn't imagine him in the job.

But what about the second part of the tweet, in which we are asked to imagine Trump doing something dangerously wrong? Doesn't that make up for the first part of the sentence?

No, it doesn't. Not even close.

Persuaders know that humans put more importance on the first part of a sentence than the second part. Our first impressions are hard to dislodge. And the first impression of those tweets—lots of them—involved imagining Trump winning the election.

But it gets worse. In many cases, the tweets asked voters to imagine President Trump while providing only a link to the punch line. People don't always click links, especially if they think they know what the link will say. And once Clinton created the "Imagine President Trump" pattern, you didn't need to click the link to know it was something negative about him. So you imagined Trump as president, as asked, and moved to the next tweet in your timeline.

I'm not done yet. Clinton's tweets also make voters "think past the sale" to a future where there is a President Trump. If you are making people wonder how Trump would perform as president, you have already sold them on the idea that he will be president. This is one of the most basic and well-known rules of persuasion.

LOVE TRUMPS HATE

One of the more notable persuasion failures from the Clinton campaign involved the slogan Love Trumps Hate. The first two thirds of the slogan is literally "Love Trump." Again, human brains put more weight on the first part of a sentence than the end. On a rational level, the sentence makes perfect sense, and it says what Trump's critics wanted it to say. But in the 3-D world of persuasion, this slogan simply told the world to either love Trump or love the things he hates, such as terrorism and bad trade deals.

Google made a similar branding mistake with its initial company slogan, "Don't Be Evil." In the 2-D world, that slogan is playful, clear, and morally appropriate. But in the 3-D world of persuasion, Google paired its brand with evil. You can't unsee the association. Worse yet, that sort of slogan gives the critics an easy target should there ever be a corporate misstep. And there are always corporate missteps when you are as large as Google. The company wisely dropped that slogan from its code of conduct in October of 2015.[3]

MAKE AMERICA SICK AGAIN

Here's another enormous persuasion problem Democrats caused for themselves in their attempt to use Trump's campaign slogan against him on the issue of health-care reform. Once again, they made the mistake of not realizing that the first impression is the only one that counts. And our first impression is Nancy Pelosi dressed like a Pepto-Bismol bottle standing next to a sign that suggests we should make America sick. Yes, the details of the sign clarify its intent to mean something else. But from a branding and persuasion perspective, this was an epic fail. So much so that many of my Twitter followers spontaneously suggested that the Mole had gotten a new assignment that involved making signs.

GODZILLA GETS IN THE GAME
(OR DOES HE?)

One of the interesting side stories of the election involved a major player in the election campaign whom I nicknamed Godzilla. I used a nickname because I wasn't yet sure the monster of persuasion whom I had in mind had really entered the fight. I thought I could see his paw print on Clinton's message by the summer of 2016, but I needed more evidence before outing Godzilla in public.

And by "Godzilla" I mean the Godzilla of influence. I'm talking about the one person on the planet who could take the flamethrower out of Trump's hand, flip it around, and turn him into an orange ember. If I was right, the election was about to become a fair fight for the first time. Without Godzilla on her side, Clinton was unarmed and helpless. Once Godzilla entered the fight, all bets were off. It was the story you didn't see on television. Not even once. And it was the only story that mattered from that point on. Everything else was second-dimension noise.

Prior to the summer of 2016, while Senator Bernie Sanders was still competing for the Democratic nomination, the Clinton persuasion game was nonexistent. I have already described her campaign's backward-persuasion tweeting and their artless campaign slogans. As far as I could tell, no one trained in persuasion was advising the Clinton team. I saw no signs of that talent whatsoever, and the signs would have been obvious to me. I told you earlier that it takes a persuader to spot a persuader. I saw nothing.

I can't say the same for the Sanders campaign. Sanders was beating expectations everywhere. He even had the best (most persuasive) television campaign ad of the election. I noted it at the time in my blog, and a Vanderbilt University study later named it the most effective ad of the election, reporting that it made people happy and hopeful.[1] The ad featured optimistic-looking people streaming toward a seaside stage to see Sanders speak, all to the tune of a patriotic song by Simon & Garfunkel, "America." It was uplifting and inspirational. It was an identity play—the strongest *positive* form of persuasion. It was right on message. It showed real persuasion talent—the kind I was not seeing from Clinton's side.

In the end, Sanders's persuasion advantage was not powerful enough to stop Clinton from winning the nomination. Clinton's fund-raising advantage and her entrenched support within the leadership of the party were too much to overcome.

Many observers were surprised how well Sanders did. Polls even said he would be the stronger candidate against Trump. That's an impressive campaign performance from a disheveled old socialist with no charisma and a budget that didn't add up. When you see someone exceed expectations by that much, it is often a sign of a Master Persuader. President Obama was a Master Persuader (or was advised by one), and he beat expectations. Bill Clinton was a Master Persuader (or was advised by one). He beat expectations too.

But Sanders was not a Master Persuader. He didn't exhibit that kind of talent in unscripted interviews. And that means he probably had a Master Persuader advising him to get the main messaging right, and perhaps the campaign ads too. There were signs of real persuasion skills all over Sanders's campaign, but none for Clinton.

That changed right after Sanders lost the nomination. But why?

If Sanders had a Master Persuader advising his team—someone such as Godzilla, for example—that adviser would have become a free agent after Clinton locked down the Democratic nomination. At about the same time, and perhaps not by coincidence, Clinton's team went from having no persuasion game at all to weapons-grade persuasion. It was a sudden change that I noticed in real time. I could see the fingerprints of one Master Persuader in particular. I figured I was seeing either the Master Persuader of all Master Persuaders—Godzilla—or perhaps one of his many protégés. All I knew for sure is that I could see Godzilla's DNA all over the Clinton messaging from the summer on.

Here's how I described it in my blog.

Posted July 24, 2016

If you are following the media coverage after the GOP convention, you know that Democrats and their surrogates are describing Trump's speech as "dark." The first ten times I heard the word, I thought it might be a situation in which someone clever used the term once and others copied it.

That is not the case.

"Dark" is a linguistic kill shot from the Left. I assume all the TV pundits on Clinton's team got the message to use the word "dark." I confess that at first I didn't recognize how good it is. It is engineered persuasion, Trump style, and it didn't come from an amateur. The Clinton team is playing some serious 3-D chess now.

Do you remember all of those policy details Clinton talked about this week? Me neither. She's done with that uselessness now. She went full Voldemort on Trump this week and unleashed a "dark" spell. It's a good one.

Let me tell you why "dark" is so good.

It's unique. That's a Trump trick. You haven't heard "dark" used before in a political context. That makes it memorable and sticky. And it brings no baggage with it to this domain because no other politician has been so labeled.

"Dark" makes you think of black, and black makes you think of racism (in the political season, anyway), and that makes you reflexively pair Trump with racism even though it makes no sense.

"Dark" can describe anything scary. It invites the listener to fill in the nightmare with whatever scares them the most about Trump. That's a hypnosis trick. Leave out the details and let people fill in the story that persuades them the most.

Repetition. "Dark" is the kind of word that pundits can work into almost any answer when talking about Trump. That means you'll hear it a lot.

I don't think this one word will change the election by much. But it's a sign that Clinton has at least one world-class persuader/adviser on the team. I have a feeling I know who. This linguistic kill shot has a partial fingerprint. If I'm right, Godzilla just got into the game.

By August I was putting a name to Godzilla because I had learned that he had advised President Obama in his 2012 campaign. When I first saw Godzilla's fingerprints on the election, I had no idea he had ever worked on a presidential campaign. But according to the *New York Times*, he had. The *New York Times* reported in November 2012, after Obama's unexpected victory:

> [The] Obama campaign also had a panel of unpaid academic advisers. The group—which calls itself the "consortium of behavioral scientists," or COBS—provided ideas on how to counter false rumors, like one that President Obama is a Muslim. It suggested how to characterize the Republican opponent, Mitt Romney, in advertisements. It also delivered research-based advice on how to mobilize voters.

The article went on to say, "The consortium included Susan T. Fiske of Princeton University; Samuel L. Popkin of the University of California, San Diego; Robert Cialdini, a professor emeritus at Arizona State University; Richard H. Thaler, a professor of behavioral science and economics at the University of Chicago's business school; and Michael Morris, a psychologist at Columbia."

There it was: Robert Cialdini. Author of the book *Influence*, the most well-known book on the power of persuasion. His new book, *Pre-Suasion*, was just hitting shelves around election day. I had an advance copy of his new book, signed and mailed to me by Cialdini himself. He was aware of my blogging on the topic of persuasion, and I assume he knew that I often recommended his book. In fact, both of his books are on my Persuasion Reading List in appendix A.

Cialdini's newer book, *Pre-Suasion*, focuses on how to prime a person to be persuaded. It teaches how to put a thought in a person's mind that will influence the next thought in ways that would not be obvious to the untrained. I mentioned earlier a study in which volunteers were shown an image of an American flag before being asked which political candidate they preferred. The volunteers who saw the American flag immediately before they were asked to pick a candidate were far more likely to prefer a Republican. That's pre-suasion: You add the influence before the question is even asked.

And that brings me back to the word "dark."

"Dark" is pre-suasion. "Dark" primes you to see whatever Trump does next as having bad intentions. "Dark" sets your brain's filter to see evil. "Dark" is not normal campaign talk. "Dark" is not even normal influence. "Dark" is pre-suasion.

"Dark" is a partial fingerprint.

"Dark" sounds like Cialdini's work.

Cialdini is Godzilla.

Am I sure? No. But I mentioned my hypothesis to a feature writer, who tried to track Cialdini down for a response. According to the writer, the response was "No comment." Which to my ears does not sound like a person who is *not* advising a candidate.

Also, people who know Cialdini personally told the writer who tracked this down that he was advising Clinton. I won't call that confirmation because I heard it from someone who heard it from someone else. But the hypothesis fits.

Coincidentally—or not—I had a few direct communications with Cialdini during the election, via Twitter direct messaging. We follow each other on Twitter, and that means we can send private messages. The messages were about his new book. He asked if he could send me a prepublication copy. This is normal business for authors. You send advance copies to anyone who might say good things about the book in public. I gave him my home address to mail it. We exchanged professional compliments. That was it.

At about the same time, Cialdini knew I was publicly naming him as Godzilla. My followers on social media were tweeting my Godzilla mentions to him. *Breitbart* ran a big article saying I had named Cialdini as a Clinton adviser. He had my contact information. He could have easily and privately told me he wasn't advising Clinton.

I never got a message of that type.

Godzilla was in the game.

Now it was a fair fight.

Over the summer of 2016, Clinton's persuasion game went from laughable to weapons grade. She painted a picture of Trump that was dark to the extreme. Clinton and her surrogates tirelessly repeated the persuasion word "dark." The word came to represent all of Trump's alleged flaws. "Dark" meant racism and authoritarianism. It meant reckless behavior. It meant inappropriate language and actions. It meant he was mentally unbalanced. It meant whatever the voters wanted it to mean, so long as it was something negative.

I taught you that the second-best form of persuasion is an appeal to *identity*. Trump was using identity to brand his campaign as a movement for all Americans. It was strong persuasion, and it was working. The only way to top identity persuasion is with the number one best persuasion form: fear.

A big fear beats every other form of persuasion. Clinton used the word

"dark" to capture all of our fears in one scary package that we couldn't forget. We're afraid of the dark, and when Clinton was done campaigning, half of the country was afraid of Trump as well. Not just a little bit afraid. Not simply concerned that his policies would be suboptimal. This was *real* fear. This was fear to the bone. And it worked. Clinton started to build a solid lead over Trump in the polls.[2]

I told you earlier in this book that Trump brought a flamethrower to a stick fight. But now Godzilla was taking sides with the sticks. Flamethrowers won't stop Godzilla. Clinton's campaign machine, combined with Godzilla's message magic, could easily be enough to take Trump out of the game unless he performed flawlessly.

Trump did not perform flawlessly, but he had a powerful set of tools, and he had momentum. By now even some of his biggest critics, such as Michael Moore, started to openly worry that he had enough persuasion power to pull off an upset.

Even against Godzilla.

HOW TO GET AWAY
WITH BAD BEHAVIOR

My mother had a favorite saying, origin unknown: "You can get used to anything if you do it long enough. Even hanging." She trotted out that saying whenever my siblings or I complained about something that wasn't going to change.

My mom's point of view captures an important rule in persuasion. People can get past minor annoyances if you give them enough time. Humans quickly adapt to just about anything that doesn't kill them.

> **PERSUASION TIP 22**
>
> People automatically get used to minor annoyances over time.

That's good news for people who have annoying habits. If you can't change your habits, acknowledge them with humor and wait for people to get used to you. If your intentions are good, sometimes that's all you need.

If your brain didn't have the ability to ignore minor annoyances, you

would have trouble functioning. Your daily experience is brimming with small annoyances. If every one of them stayed at the top of your priority list, you wouldn't be able to get anything done. One of your brain's best features is its ability to automatically get over your smaller problems so you can focus on your bigger ones.

You see this dynamic most vividly in your personal life. When a small misunderstanding between you and a loved one plunges you into an angry mood, the bad feeling starts to wear off in a few days even if nothing changes but the passage of time. The human mind is designed to "get over it" whenever the stakes are not high. And the stakes are not high for most of what we do.

This rule of persuasion helped me predict a Trump presidency a year before most observers could see it as a possibility. The most common objection I heard when Trump first announced his run was that people simply could not wrap their heads around the possibility that this obnoxious monster could ever be acceptable to enough voters to become president. Most people probably assumed their initial opinions of Trump would remain stable. As a trained persuader, I assumed the *opposite*, because people can get used to anything if they do it long enough. I could see from the start of the election that for many people Trump's personal style was annoying to the point of painful. I also knew the public would have a full year to get used to his personality. And I knew that the longer they experienced it, the less outrageous it would seem—at least for some portion of the public. Others would harden their resistance. But the latter group was never going to vote for Trump anyway. The people who mattered were the ones who disliked his style but didn't yet have a final opinion about his politics. That group was going to get used to Trump's personality over time. It was inevitable. That's how our brains are wired. For most people, novelty wears off. To be fair, some people will get *more* bothered by Trump's personality over time. But as I said, people who had super hardened hate for Trump at the start were unlikely to vote for him anyway.

As I mentioned earlier in the book, one advantage I had as a Trump observer was that I grew up in New York. But I've lived my adult life in California, and that gives me a basis for comparison. One of the big

differences between those two states is that the residents appear to have
different senses of humor. Take, for example, Trump's comment about
Senator John McCain's war record. During an interview on July 18, 2015,
at the Family Leadership Summit, Trump dismissed McCain's criticisms
by joking that he prefers veterans who "weren't captured." A lot of people
found that comment offensive. I think some people didn't even recognize
it as a joke. And even if voters did see it as a joke, many considered it deeply
offensive to Senator McCain, to veterans, and even to America.

But let me teach you something about a New York sense of humor. If
you don't understand what New Yorkers think is funny, Trump looks like
a monster. From a California perspective, Trump's comments about Mc-
Cain are deeply disturbing. That's because Californians put the wrong
frame on it. I'll fix that for you right now. Here's what you need to know
about a New York sense of humor. (And obviously this is a generality that
won't apply to all.)

When we current or ex–New Yorkers laugh at "offensive" jokes, we are
usually reacting to the *awfulness* of it. We are *not laughing at the target* of
the joke. (Again, this is a generality.) Trump's quip about preferring veterans who didn't get caught is a perfect example. It's funny *because* the idea
is so awful. In other words, the person telling the offensive joke and the
person offended by the joke are *on exactly the same side*. An average New
Yorker thinks the *inappropriateness* of the joke is what makes it funny,
whereas the Californian sees it as an attack on the individual—in this
case, a highly respected veteran. I saw Trump's joke as a playful response
and the type of thing he might say to his best friend. Californians saw a
monster acting like a monster. Same world, different movies.

I should also note that Trump's joke about preferring veterans who
didn't get caught is a standard joke formula. My best guess is that he recognized the joke setup and it was too juicy to
pass up. He probably also had a New Yorker's
blind spot to how that joke would be seen by
the rest of the country. The thing that protected Trump from this joke becoming a bigger problem was that he had a strong record of

PERSUASION TIP 23

What you say is important,
but it is never as
important as what people
think you are thinking.

backing veterans, and he continued to strengthen that association during the campaign. All communication depends on what we believe is in the mind of the person communicating. We believed Trump was sincere about his concern for veterans, and so he got a bit of a free pass for his offensive joke.

Here's how I described the New York personality in my blog, two months after Trump announced his candidacy.

Posted August 5, 2015

The visceral reaction that makes so many people dislike Trump has a lot to do with his New York style. I grew up in upstate New York, and his style registers with me in a completely different way than it does with my California friends who can't stand him. What I see is bluntness, honesty, some risk taking, and a competitive nature. I don't hate any of that. In fact, I kind of like it.

I have blogged about making the transition from my New York personality to my California personality. New Yorkers tend to say whatever they think is true to whoever is standing nearby. Not much filter. Californians say what they think will make you feel good. The California way would feel like lying if it were not so well-meaning.

I certainly understand that Trump comes off as arrogant, obnoxious, and lots of other bad stuff. But over time, and compared with the liars onstage with him, you might get hooked on hearing his honest* opinions. That's how the New York style works. At first you hate it because it seems so harsh. In time, you start to

---

*By "honest" I mean emotionally and directionally. I think we all agree he exhausts the fact-checkers on the stuff that apparently isn't important enough to prevent one from becoming president.

appreciate the honesty. And when you realize the harshness is not a signal of real evil—just a style—you tend to get over it. He won't win over all of his haters, but I predict that his New York style will grow on people more than you would expect. You could say his style is his biggest problem, but it might be self-solving with time and exposure. He is getting both.

HOW A TRAINED PERSUADER
EVALUATES SCANDALS

n this chapter I evaluate the influence on voters of the fresher scandals that arose during the campaign. My opinions here are closer to art than science, since I have no way to measure the impact of any specific influence. If you asked voters which scandals changed their votes, they might give you confident answers, but you shouldn't trust them. In emotion-charged situations such as elections, we decide first and rationalize later. Any poll on this topic would detect voter rationalizations, nothing more.

With that caveat, I think you might find it useful to see how a trained persuader evaluates scandals for their likely impact. Let's look at a few.

TRUMP'S TAXES

For decades, candidates for president of the United States regularly released their tax returns so voters could look for any signs of conflict of interest or wrongdoing.[1] Trump broke with tradition by saying he would not release his returns, citing as his reason that he was under audit and things could change. Critics assumed he was hiding something important. Supporters either believed his tax returns were irrelevant or preferred that they stay hidden so Trump could prevail.

Persuasion-wise, Trump allowed opponents to imagine there were some bad things in his tax returns. That would be terrible persuasion technique unless the alternative is to give critics dozens of fresh targets—both real and imagined—by releasing the details.

The public at large is not savvy about business or corporate taxes. Trump's critics would have cherry-picked elements from his returns and framed them as the work of a crook, even if they were legal. In the event that the IRS agreed that Trump's tax strategies followed the law, critics could still find evidence on the returns that Trump was an ungenerous weasel. There was no way for Trump to win by releasing his tax returns.

Voters probably hate the IRS as much as Trump's critics disliked Trump. And every taxpayer uses every available strategy to reduce taxes. On one hand, the unknowns about Trump's taxes were worrisome. But that persuasion had no visual power and did not evoke any concrete fears, ones that went beyond the conceptual. On the other hand, a little bit of "fudging" on taxes probably made Trump more relatable to taxpayers accustomed to doing the same.

Overall, I think the persuasion impact of Trump's taxes was low, especially in the context of so many other provocations and scandals that were visual and far juicier.

KKK SLOW DENIAL

February 2016

In a televised interview with CNN's Jake Tapper, Trump stumbled and hesitated on a question about disavowing the KKK and its former grand wizard, David Duke. Both had recently endorsed his campaign. Trump later claimed he had a defective earpiece and didn't hear the question clearly. Critics said his hesitation to disavow was a clear sign that he was a racist. This event more than any other added fodder to the allegations that Trump is a racist.

For context, you should know that Trump had disavowed David Duke a number of times in the past, and the day after the Tapper interview he clearly disavowed both Duke and the KKK. He left no wiggle room.

The Tapper interview went like this.

Tapper: I want to ask you about the Anti-Defamation League, which this week called on you to publicly condemn unequivocally the racism of former KKK grand wizard David Duke, who recently said that voting against you at this point would be treason to your heritage.

Will you unequivocally condemn David Duke and say that you don't want his vote or that of other white supremacists in this election?

Trump: Well, just so you understand, I don't know anything about David Duke. Okay? I don't know anything about what you're even talking about with white supremacy or white supremacists. So, I don't know.

I don't know, did he endorse me or what's going on, because, you know, I know nothing about David Duke. I know nothing about white supremacists. And so you're asking me a question that I'm supposed to be talking about people that I know nothing about.

Tapper: But I guess the question from the Anti-Defamation League is, even if you don't know about their endorsement, there are these groups and individuals endorsing you. Would you just say unequivocally you condemn them and you don't want their support?

Trump: Well, I have to look at the group. I mean, I don't know what group you're talking about.

You wouldn't want me to condemn a group that I know nothing about. I would have to look. If you would send me a list of the groups, I will do research on them. And, certainly, I would disavow if I thought there was something wrong.

Tapper: The Ku Klux Klan?

Trump: But you may have groups in there that are totally fine, and it would be very unfair. So, give me a list of the groups, and I will let you know.

Tapper: Okay. I mean, I'm just talking about David Duke and the Ku Klux Klan here, but . . .

Trump: I don't know any—honestly, I don't know David Duke. I don't believe I have ever met him. I'm pretty sure I didn't meet him. And I just don't know anything about him.

Persuasion-wise, this was probably Trump's biggest error of the campaign. When you see the interview live, or read the transcript, it does make you wonder what the heck he was thinking. But the one thing I feel comfortable saying is that he wasn't planning to embrace the KKK and its past leader while running for president of the United States. That doesn't make sense in any world in which Trump is sane. And I think he is sane.

Trump's claim of a faulty earpiece probably sounds ridiculous to you. But I can tell you, from my own experience with hundreds of similar interviews, the connection is often bad, and you don't realize how bad until you are in the interview. I can confirm that I have done live television interviews by satellite and found myself literally guessing what the question was because of a faulty connection. Far more times I have asked the engineer at the remote studio to try connecting on another line because the sound on the first one was unclear. So a "bad earpiece" is fairly common, assuming that is shorthand for any problem with the sound.

In the 2-D world where facts and logic matter, I found Trump's explanation of a bad earpiece to be plausible, assuming he was referring to bad sound quality in general. But in the 3-D world of persuasion, this was his biggest campaign error. Even if you allow that he had trouble hearing the questions, it was a persuasion mistake to say he didn't know enough about David Duke to disavow him. My best guess is that Trump was being consistent with his practice of never giving away anything until he can trade it for value. He needed every vote he could get, including votes from people who think and do things you and I don't like. If that sounds terrible to you, keep in mind that Trump's background is the construction business in New York. He has dealt with unsavory characters. And sometimes those unsavory characters are a small part of a larger plan for a greater good, whether you hate them or not. You can make up your own mind about the ethics of using bad people to get good outcomes.

This scandal was sticky because it played to the confirmation bias that Trump is a racist. And it fit nicely on the laundry list of "evidence" that Trump was up to something "dark." This scandal probably changed some votes.

JUDGE CURIEL

June 2016

The Trump University case ended up in the court of Judge Gonzalo Curiel, an American citizen with Mexican-born parents. Trump complained that the judge might be biased because, as Trump put it, the judge is "Mexican." This characterization was important to Trump because his flagship policy involved getting tough on illegal Mexican immigrants, and that made him deeply unpopular with Americans of Mexican heritage.

In the context of a legal case, lawyers routinely look for bias by association and try to limit it to achieve a fair trial. That's why judges recuse themselves when there is either potential bias or the appearance of it. Most people agree with the idea that humans have bias, but when the concept is extended to include ethnicity as a variable, it violates our most basic instincts of fairness.

Critics decried Trump's characterization of the judge as "Mexican," saying it was both inaccurate and racist because the judge is an American citizen. Trump's critics did a solid job of overinterpreting Trump's comments to mean he was saying Mexicans in general are not capable of being fair judges. (Trump didn't say that.)

To give this topic some context, ask any of your American friends of Italian heritage to describe their families. There's a good chance they will refer to themselves as "Italian." Ask any American-born friend with Mexican heritage to describe himself and there's a good chance he will use the descriptor "Mexican." Americans use this sort of shorthand all the time. Citizenship is a separate question.

My opinion on the Judge Curiel scandal is that Trump was using a shorthand way of describing a potential source of bias. I doubt Trump was questioning the judge's citizenship. I think he was reminding us that it would be hard for Judge Curiel to rule in favor of Trump and still feel okay at the next Curiel family gathering. All humans have bias, and family-related bias is among our strongest instincts.

Judges are trained to think past their biases and apply the law. But judges are also human, so they can't be expected to be biasfree simply because they are trained to act that way.

Trump's outrageous claim that Judge Curiel might be biased because of his Mexican heritage was good legal strategy, in my opinion, albeit clumsily done. It created two potential outcomes. Either the judge would rule in Trump's favor, or the groundwork had been laid for Trump to claim he lost only because of a biased judge.

Trump made a bad persuasion mistake when he referred to the judge as "Mexican" instead of calling him an American with Mexican heritage. But that mistake was somewhat balanced by the fact that he might have persuaded the judge to be extra fair to him or else be forever labeled biased.

Judge Curiel signaled that he planned to schedule the court case for the summer or early fall of 2016. The timing would have been terrible for Trump's campaign. The dusty old Trump University scandal would have rapidly evolved into a new scandal in voters' minds, complete with lots of visuals, details, and alleged victims. It could have been a disaster.

Trump's lawyers argued for a delay until after the election. The judge was under no obligation to grant the delay. One could argue that he had a greater obligation to *not* treat Trump as special. There was no legal basis for granting a delay.

Judge Curiel granted the delay. And it probably saved the election for Trump.

You can say Trump made a mistake when he called out Judge Curiel's potential bias by association. He definitely made a big mistake in the way he worded his objection. But Trump also made it nearly impossible for the judge to rule against Trump in any gray area. The court date was a gray area, and a judgment call. It went Trump's way.

My best guess is that the net persuasion effect of this entire situation was positive for Trump. On one hand, it was a mistake to use the term "Mexican" as a shorthand for Mexican heritage and give his critics so much ammunition. But at the same time, Trump removed bigger weapons from his critics by taking the Trump University court case out of the election cycle. I think Trump actually won that chess game, but clumsily so. And it came with a big cost in his reputation for being "dark."

Update: Tonight at dinner a young man at my table who was born and raised in America referred to himself as "Mexican" because he is 20 percent Hispanic by way of Mexico. Candidate Trump was talking about Judge Curiel the way normal people talk about themselves in casual conversations.

KHAN CONTROVERSY

July 2016

At the Democratic National Convention in Philadelphia, a Muslim American lawyer named Khizr Khan spoke movingly about how his son, an army captain, died a hero in 2004 in Iraq. The larger context of the speech involved pointed criticism of Trump and his policies.

Asked about Mr. Khan's speech, Trump told ABC's George Stephanopoulos that Mr. Khan seemed like a "nice guy," but he wondered aloud why Khan's wife stood next to him and didn't speak. Trump said, "If you look at his wife, she was standing there, she had nothing to say, she probably—maybe she wasn't allowed to have anything to say, you tell me."

Trump's implication was that the Khans' religion stifles the free expression of women. Trump's supporters probably found it amusing and on point. His critics called it racist and sexist and said he disrespected the parents of a fallen hero.

This is another example of how Trump sometimes makes an unforced error that has the effect of making voters focus where he wants them to focus. In this case, Trump wanted voters to believe Muslim immigration could bring with it some unpopular attitudes about gender. As long as people were thinking about that issue, Trump had an edge.

Unfortunately for Trump, this controversy fit nicely with Clinton's "dark" persuasion and added to the confirmation bias. But Trump took some of the energy out of this scandal by using it to frame immigration as dangerous for women. Both sides used fear persuasion, but Clinton probably got the best of the exchange because her persuasion was a twofer: It painted Trump as disrespectful to a fallen military hero as well as racist.

Trump was somewhat protected from the criticism that he was disrespectful to a fallen military hero because he had done a great job of focusing on veterans' issues during the campaign. This scandal probably didn't change many votes.

ANTHONY WEINER'S LAPTOP

August 2016

Anthony Weiner was the husband of Hillary Clinton's closest adviser, Huma Abedin. Weiner allegedly got caught more than once sexting with women who were not his wife, including a teen girl.

I will skip the details.

Trump supporters tried with some success to put the stink of that scandal on Hillary Clinton by association. But Huma quietly left the campaign, and other scandals pushed this one off the top of the news. This one didn't do much damage, in my opinion. But it might have made Trump's upcoming Pussygate scandal less damaging because it lessened the contrast between Trump's bad behavior and Hillary Clinton's reputation by association.

BASKET OF DEPLORABLES

September 2016

Speaking at the LGBT for Hillary gala in New York City on September 9, 2016, Hillary Clinton said that half of Trump's supporters were "racist, sexist, homophobic, xenophobic, Islamophobic." She went on to call them a "basket of deplorables." Trump responded by saying Clinton's remarks showed "her true *contempt* for everyday Americans."

Marriage experts will tell you that the best indicator of a future divorce is when the couple displays *contempt* for each other. Couples can get past most other types of problems with some work. But contempt is a reliable signal that a relationship is in serious trouble, say the experts.[2]

Hillary Clinton had just shown contempt for a large portion of the electorate. Trump, the Master Persuader, probably considered all of the ways he might frame Clinton's "deplorables" comment for political advantage. He could have said it was awful, inappropriate, insulting, sick, or any one of dozens of descriptors. But he didn't. He reached into the third dimension and plucked out the *one* word with the absolute strongest persuasion power: "contempt."

I don't have to tell you that the English language contains lots of words. But there was only one *best* word for this situation. Trump probably found it. He once famously said he "has the best words." In the second dimension, that claim is false. In the third dimension, Trump does indeed have the best words. He proved it once again with his choice of the word "contempt."

It was perfect. And it wasn't luck.

After the election, Clinton's "deplorables" speech was often mentioned on social media as a reason that people voted for Trump. In the 2-D world, that would seem to make sense. But in the 3-D world of persuasion, the "deplorables" comment might have been what I call a "fake because." In other words, it was a rationalization for what people wanted to do anyway. History will record that the "deplorables" comment might have changed the election. The Persuasion Filter agrees it *might* have, but it also might have simply given Trump supporters cover for the vote they wanted to cast anyway.

Soon after the "deplorables" comment, I got on a Periscope live stream and noted that many Trump supporters were deplorable, sure, but they were "adorable deplorables."

"Adorable deplorables" became one of the many positive spins that Trump supporters put on Clinton's contemptuous comment. The "deplorables" insult turned into memes and clothing for Trump supporters, and it happened within hours.

Clinton's "deplorables" comment was a persuasion mistake of epic proportions. It validated what many Trump supporters suspected: Clinton didn't simply disagree with Republicans; she literally had no respect for a large percentage of them. And that doesn't work if you are running to be the leader of the entire country.

WIKILEAKS, CLINTON, COMEY, AND RUSSIA

This scandal had its roots before the election. I'll show you the time line, for context, before we get to the fresh stuff.

In March 2015, during Hillary Clinton's tenure as secretary of state, she used her private e-mail server for official communications. Those official communications included thousands of e-mails that would retroactively be marked "classified" by the State Department.

On July 5, 2016, FBI Director Comey announced that the FBI's investigation had concluded that Clinton was "extremely careless" in handling her e-mail system but recommended that no charges be filed against her.

On July 6, 2016, Attorney General Loretta Lynch announced that no charges would be filed.

On October 28, 2016, Comey notified Congress that the FBI had started looking into newly discovered e-mails found on a laptop belonging to Clinton aide Huma Abedin's husband, Anthony Weiner, during an investigation of his sexting scandals.

On November 6, 2016, Comey notified Congress that the FBI had not changed its conclusion, reached in July, regarding Clinton's e-mails.

Over the summer of 2016, Wikileaks teased that it had access to e-mails from the Democratic National Committee's e-mail server with explosive revelations. Wikileaks trickled out the e-mails in small batches to keep the public engaged.

The worst thing we heard (that was credible) from the hacked DNC e-mails was that Clinton supporter and CNN pundit Donna Brazile had shared an upcoming primary debate question with candidate Clinton. As bombshells go, that was a small one. But it did add fuel to Trump's claim that the media was against him.

The hacked DNC e-mails also sparked the so-called Pizzagate allegation that high-ranking Democrats were engaged in a cult that involved satanic worship, sexual abuse of children, and pizza. This story got a lot of attention, but it probably didn't achieve enough credibility to influence many votes. Personally, I didn't believe any of it.

Clinton's e-mail scandal was confusing to the public, and I think it got conflated in people's minds with the alleged Russian hacking of the DNC's e-mail server that got released to Wikileaks. Add all of that to the Clinton Foundation allegations, and the public started feeling as if something wasn't quite right with the Clintons. Trump helped that impression along with his branding of Hillary Clinton as crooked. The public heard complicated news reports they didn't understand, but it looked to them as if they were seeing plenty of smoke, so there must be fire.

Notice how "crooked" became a sponge for soaking up confirmation bias. It worked as well as "dark" worked on the other side. Both are examples of weapons-grade persuasion.

Hillary Clinton and her supporters, along with many pundits and voters, believe that Comey's reopening of the e-mail investigation because of new e-mails found on Weiner's laptop cost Clinton the election. Clinton's poll numbers dropped right after the Comey announcement. But in the third dimension, Comey's actions were probably a "fake because" that people used to vote the way they had already decided to vote. In my opinion, Comey was not hugely influential to the outcome. But history will probably say he was.

MISS UNIVERSE CONTROVERSY

September 2016

Hillary Clinton mentioned in a presidential debate that back in 1996 Trump had called a Miss Universe winner, Alicia Machado, "Miss Piggy" because of her weight gain. Trump owned the Miss Universe contest in those days, and when his winner gained weight, it was problematic for the brand. As we later learned, Trump was flexible with Machado at the time and tried to work with her to keep her title and support her in losing weight. But Trump's critics characterized him as being disrespectful to women.

Trump's supporters didn't find this issue terribly important because they figured a spokesperson for a beauty contest probably has some responsibility to stay in shape. And they weren't bothered by any politically incorrect things said about the issue.

Clinton's supporters found in this one more bit of evidence (or confirmation bias) for Trump's general awfulness. But I doubt this scandal changed many votes, if any.

PUSSYGATE: THE *ACCESS HOLLYWOOD* RECORDING

October 2016

A month before election day, the *Washington Post* released an audio recording in which Trump and television host Billy Bush had a lewd private conversation about women in 2005. Both men were wearing microphones for an upcoming TV segment and didn't realize they were being recorded.

In the audio, Trump boasted about his star appeal and its effect on women, saying, "I don't even wait. And when you're a star, they let you do it. You can do anything. . . . Grab them by the pussy."

Trump's critics and other observers described Trump's statements as confessions of sexual abuse. Trump's supporters dismissed it as meaningless "locker room talk." Trump issued a statement apologizing for the audio's content in which he reduced its power by adding a contrast adjustment. He said Bill Clinton had "said far worse to me on the golf course."

This was the most damaging scandal for Trump. It erupted only a month before election day, so the timing was ideal for the Clinton camp. It had a strong visual component, both because we saw video of Trump with Billy Bush after the comments and because we reflexively imagine Trump grabbing a woman in an inappropriate way. And it fit into the "dark" framing with the rest of Trump's alleged bad behavior.

But it wasn't entirely bad, for a reason that isn't obvious in the second dimension. Until this scandal broke, the main objection to Trump was that he was literally a Hitler-like strongman leader in waiting. The *Access Hollywood* tape had the unintended effect of humanizing Trump and taking people's minds from the Hitler frame to the "flawed guy" frame.

Had the *Access Hollywood* tape been the only scandal of the campaign, it might have been decisive. But in the context of a Trump-is-Hitler framing, it may have taken some of the scare off of him by moving people's impression of him from Hitler-like strongman to flawed male. That's a promotion.

As bad as the scandal was, I find it hard to know for sure whether it helped Trump or hurt him. My best guess is that it cost him votes, but it was less of a problem than people assumed it would be. Part of what protected Trump from that scandal is that some form of bad-boy sexual behavior was already baked into what we assumed about him. He never presented himself as an angel. It would have been a fatal mistake if he had.

If you look at the scandals individually, they seem like the types of things that can move elections. But collectively they involve too much information for voters to process. So instead, voters likely defaulted to their biases. Both candidates created plenty of fodder for confirmation bias. Clinton's scandals made her look more "crooked" every day, while Trump's scandals contributed to his "dark" reputation. The main standout among the scandals, in my opinion, was Clinton's "deplorables" speech. Voters expect a certain amount of sketchy behavior from their leaders and discount it in their minds. But no one discounts contempt when they hear it.

HOW TO WIN BY A HAIR(CUT)

From a persuasion perspective, we can't ignore President Trump's famous haircut and what I assume was a fake tan of some sort. Early on in the race, both his hair and face registered in our minds as orange. And that's a problem if you are trying to be taken seriously as a representative of the country. But like many problems, this one presented an opportunity. Trump could solve his distracting haircut and his oversized ego with one simple act: He could shave his head. I whimsically but seriously suggested exactly that, more than a year before election day.

On August 5, 2015, I blogged . . .

If Trump wants the independents and some Democrats to vote his way, he needs something bigger. He needs a trump card.

And he has it.

His hair.

I believe Donald Trump could become president of the United States if he promised to shave his head upon winning. Or perhaps he could do it a month before the election to suck all the media attention from his competitor.

Right. Think about it. Voters are emotional creatures and they
would love such an act of humility coming from such an egotistical
jerk. People love to see other people change. That is the formula for
successful movies: The protagonist changes when the audience
thinks such change is not possible. We LOVE that.

As it turned out, Trump did not need to shave his head to win. But he
did improve his haircut during the campaign. And it looks like he dyed it
a blonder shade. He also fixed his fake tan, or whatever was making him
orange. Today you don't see the orange. I think this slow transformation
was a big help in his win. We like to think we are rational voters, but that
haircut in its severe original form would have scared people away. Trump
solved that (to some extent), as Master Persuaders do. By election day the
nonstop ridicule of Trump's hair had slowed to nearly nothing. We got
used to his appearance, while at the same time he evolved to a less distracting look. Most people probably didn't notice the change.

HOW TO CREATE TWO WAYS TO WIN, NO WAY TO LOSE

O ne of Trump's most entertaining persuasion strategies is what I call "Two Ways to Win, No Way to Lose." I'll give you some examples.

In January of 2016, Iran briefly detained ten American sailors for entering Iranian waters. Candidate Trump cleverly staked out the position that if Iran didn't release the sailors soon, he would make Iran pay for its treachery when he became president. With this setup, one of two things could happen:

- Iran might keep the sailors in custody through the election, allowing Trump to use it as an example of why American voters need to elect a badass, such as Trump, to deal with Iran, or . . .
- Iran might release the sailors before the election, and Trump could claim it did so because of his tough talk.

Iran released the sailors fifteen hours after they were captured. Trump immediately suggested that his tough talk had made a difference.

In an earlier chapter, I talked about Trump using the two-ways-to-win technique with his criticism of the judge in his Trump University case. By questioning the judge's impartiality before the case was heard, Trump created two ways to win:

- Trump's accusation of bias could cause the judge to overcompensate to avoid the *appearance* of bias and rule in Trump's favor, or . . .
- If Trump didn't get the verdict he wanted, he could later claim the reason was the judge's bias.

Trump fumbled on this play by referring to the judge as "Mexican." But that is a separate issue. His two-ways-to-win strategy would have been a solid approach had he avoided that unforced error.

As I write this chapter, Speaker of the House of Representatives Paul Ryan is taking the lead in putting together a first pass of a health-care bill that is intended to replace Obamacare. Trump is being hands off on the details, allowing Ryan to get branded with whatever plans come out of the first few iterations and negotiations. One of two things can happen:

- Ryan succeeds with a health-care bill that is surprisingly bipartisan, and the country feels it is an improvement over Obamacare (in which case the Trump administration looks great; presidents take credit for good things that happen during their administrations), or . . .

- Ryan's plans fail miserably in the court of public opinion. In that case, President Trump can step in and start moving both sides to the middle. The Republicans would be softened up by their recent failure, and Democrats would be scared to death that their only options are the stingy Republican plan that doesn't cover enough people and no health-care plan at all. Having softened up both sides, Trump gives himself room to find the middle.

At this writing, I am not predicting that Trump will easily swoop in and find a middle path for health care that gets enough votes to pass. I'm suggesting that the *only way a compromise health-care bill is possible* is if Trump lets Ryan go first and fail hard, while scaring the bejeezus out of the Democrats at the same time. In this context, the two ways to win are the passing of a Ryan bill that is surprisingly bipartisan and the softening up of both sides to make the middle easier to find.

For your reference, I wrote this chapter in March of 2017. By the time you read it, you'll know how things are unfolding.

Much of Trump's business revenue comes from licensing the Trump name to various products and projects. License deals are unique in the sense that they give you two ways to win and (almost) no way to lose. That's because license deals generally have some big up-front payments that are guaranteed at the signing of the deal, with potential for more fees if the business or project is profitable. That looks like this:

- If the business that licenses Trump's name fails, Trump's company keeps all the license payments that have been paid so far (and that typically includes a large up-front payment), or . . .
- If the business succeeds, Trump's company makes even more money because the license continues to pay out as a percentage of profits.

I have done similar licensing deals for *Dilbert* products for years, and for the same reason. Similarly, as an established author, I also get paid for my books before I write them. If the book does poorly, I keep the large up-front advance. If the book is a huge best seller, I make even more money in ongoing royalties. I have two ways to win and no way to lose.

When Trump dabbled in running for president in prior election cycles, he also had two ways to win and no way to lose. If he didn't get any traction in the polls, he still raised his profile and the value of his brand. In his earlier flirtations with running for president, you didn't see him being so provocative with his policies as he was with his successful run in 2016. The earlier efforts were low-risk, high-reward plays. By "losing" early in prior election cycles, he still put his name in everyone's mind for the next time. He was literally winning by losing.

When candidate Trump announced his candidacy in 2015, he didn't play it safe. He went the opposite direction. This created the impression that he had only one way to win. He had to get elected president, or else he would get nothing out of the exercise but a tainted reputation, thanks to his enemies branding him as a racist for his immigration proposals. But at age seventy, Trump's objectives in life appear to be more focused on the public good (believe it or not). I have heard this from reliable sources. If those insider accounts are accurate, Trump gave himself two ways to win and no way to lose, at least in terms of the public good as he sees it. It looks like this:

- If Trump lost the election, he would still influence the public's perception about the importance of border security. If we assume Trump is sincere about better border security being a public necessity, he wins by making it a more prominent issue in our minds. In this scenario, the Trump brand might suffer in the short run, but it would also likely recover.

- If Trump won the election, which he did, he would get to influence the country more directly.

In the interest of clarity, I'll acknowledge that "no way to lose" isn't an absolute. Life can always find a way to trip you up. But if you are playing the odds, always look for situations that give you two ways to win and *almost* no way to lose.

I sometimes describe this situation in a more generic sense as having a system instead of a goal. A goal is, by definition, one way to win and infinite ways to lose. A good system gives you lots of ways to win and far fewer ways to fail. An example of a good system is going to college and getting an engineering degree. You don't yet know what your ultimate career will be, but the engineering degree gives you lots of ways to win while vastly reducing the number of ways to lose. You don't see many homeless engineers. And if you do, it involves substance abuse or mental issues.

I write in detail about the advantage of systems over goals in my book *How to Fail at Almost Everything and Still Win Big*.

The next time you are in a discussion about strategy, either in business or in your personal life, listen to everyone else's suggestions and then top them with a "two ways to win, no way to lose" play, assuming your situation allows for that. You'll find that it ends every strategy discussion. No one picks one way to win and infinite ways to lose if they have an option of two ways to win and no way to lose.

PERSUASION TIP 24

If you can frame your preferred strategy as two ways to win and no way to lose, almost no one will disagree with your suggested path because it is a natural High-Ground Maneuver.

HOW TO USE THE HIGH-GROUND MANEUVER

f you have siblings, or you have more than one child of your own, you know kids like to use the "fairness" argument to get whatever their siblings already got. Most parents cave in and try to balance things right away. That's like arming a child with a powerful persuasion weapon. The kid will trot out the fairness argument at every opportunity.

My mother had a different approach. When my siblings or I complained about the unfairness of one thing or another, she would tell us bluntly that "life isn't fair." End of story. We were disarmed before the first shot was fired. That method is what I call the High-Ground Maneuver. It takes the debate out of the details—the weeds, I call them—and elevates it to the high ground where there is no disagreement. On the next page you can see how I wrote about the High-Ground Maneuver in 2010, right after Apple had its famous "Antennaegate" public relations fiasco. Watch Steve Jobs take the high ground. This is magnificent persuasion.

Posted July 19, 2010

I'm sure you're all following the iPhone 4 story. If you hold the phone a certain way, it drops calls.

In a press conference on the subject, Steve Jobs said, "We're not perfect. Phones are not perfect. We all know that. But we want to make our users happy."

Jobs got a lot of heat about his response. Where was the apology? Where was the part where he acknowledged that the buck stops with him, and that Apple made a big mistake that never should have happened? That's Public Relations 101, right?

I'm a student of how language influences people. Apple's response to the iPhone 4 problem didn't follow the public relations playbook because Jobs decided to rewrite the playbook. (I pause now to insert the necessary phrase "magnificent bastard.") If you want to know what genius looks like, study Jobs's words: "We're not perfect. Phones are not perfect. We all know that. But we want to make our users happy."

Jobs changed the entire argument with nineteen words. He was brief. He spoke indisputable truth. And later in his press conference, he offered clear fixes.

Did it work? Check out the media response. There's lots of talk about whether other smartphones are perfect or not. There's lots of talk about whether Jobs's response was the right one. But the central question that was in everyone's head before the press conference—"Is the iPhone 4 a dud?"—has, well, evaporated. Part of the change in attitude is because the fixes Apple offered are adequate. But those fixes easily could have become part of the joke if handled in an apologetic "please kick me" way.

If Jobs had not changed the context from the iPhone 4 in particular to all smartphones in general, I could make you a hilarious comic strip about a product so poorly made that it won't work if it comes in contact with a human hand. But as soon as the context is changed to "all smartphones have problems," the humor opportunity is gone. Nothing kills humor like a general and boring truth.

I've wondered for some time if Jobs studied hypnosis or if he's some sort of freakish natural. And I wonder how much of his language is planned versus off-the-cuff. He speaks and acts like a master hypnotist. (For new readers, I'm a trained hypnotist myself, and it definitely takes one to know one.)

I have long had a name for Jobs's clever move. I call it the "High-Ground Maneuver." I first noticed an executive using it years ago, and I've since used it a number of times when the situation called for it. The move involves taking an argument up to a level where you can say something that is absolutely true while changing the context at the same time. Once the move has been executed, the other participants will fear appearing small-minded if they drag the argument back to the detail level. It's an instant game changer.

For example, if a military drone accidentally kills civilians, and there is a public outcry, it would be a mistake for the military to spend too much time talking about what went wrong with that particular mission. The High-Ground Maneuver would go something like this: "War is messy. No one wants civilians to die. We will study this situation to see how we can better avoid it in the future."

Notice that the response is succinct and indisputably true and that the context has been taken to a higher level, about war in general. That's what Jobs did. It's a powerful technique, and you can use it at home.

There's a limit to the method. I don't think that BP could have gotten away with it as a response to the oil spill because the problem was so large and it seemed unique to BP. But if they had tried the High-Ground Maneuver, it would have looked like this: "All of the easy sources of oil had been found by fifty years ago. If the oil industry stops taking risks, many of you would be out of work in less than a decade. We all want a future of clean energy, but no one sees a way to get there as quickly as we need to. We will do everything we can to clean up the spill and to make things right with the gulf economy."

Someday business students will read about Steve Jobs's response to the iPhone 4 issue and they will learn that the High-Ground Maneuver (probably by some other name) became the public relations standard for consumer-products companies from that day on.

Did I read too much into Jobs's handling of this customer-relations nightmare? It's possible. But if you read the Walter Isaacson biography *Jobs,* you'll discover that Jobs personally forwarded my blog post to his subordinates. I don't think he would have done that if he thought I was wrong.

A GRAB BAG OF TRUMP'S QUICKEST AND EASIEST PERSUASION TOOLS

n this chapter I will give you a quick summary of some of Trump's persuasion tools that don't fit into any other chapter.

SOCIAL PROOF ("MANY PEOPLE ARE SAYING . . .")

Trump likes to tell us that many people agree with whatever he's telling us at the moment. That's an example of "social proof" persuasion. Humans are wired to assume that if lots of people are saying the same thing, it must be true. In Trump's case, he probably exaggerates the number of people who are agreeing with him. But the exaggerations don't hurt him. If you are skeptical of his claim that others agree with him, and you look into it, you'll certainly find *some* people who agree with him. And that's enough to bias your mind in that direction. At the very least, it tells you that other reasonable people see things the way he does.

Trump didn't have credibility with the entire country when he was campaigning, and he still doesn't. So it helps him to frame himself as the one agreeing with the majority instead of coming up with questionable opinions on his own.

ASK DIRECTLY FOR WHAT YOU WANT ("BELIEVE ME . . .")

Trump likes to punctuate the ends of his statements with "believe me." That's a direct command disguised as throwaway words. One of the rules of selling is that at some point in the pitch you have to directly ask for what you want. Trump wants you to believe him. So he asks directly. That seems like no big deal until you realize how easy it would be for him to *not* ask people to believe him. That's how most politicians operate. They say what they want to say and then they hope you believe it. Trump takes it one step further, using perfect persuasion technique, and directly asks you to believe him.

This form of persuasion isn't one of the most powerful. But keep in mind that campaigning is about finding ten messages that move one half of 1 percent of voters your way per message.

> **PERSUASION TIP 25**
>
> If you are selling, ask your potential customer to buy. Direct requests are persuasive.

REPETITION ("IT'S TRUE. IT'S TRUE.")

Trump sometimes ends his statements by saying, "It's true. It's true." That's because repetition is persuasion. If you frequently hear that a thing is true, it biases you to think there might be something to it.

> **PERSUASION TIP 26**
>
> Repetition is persuasion. Also, repetition is persuasion. And have I mentioned that repetition is persuasion?

SIMPLICITY

At the start of Trump's campaign, the critics were vicious in attacking his seemingly limited vocabulary and his simple statements. Journalists wrote stories that described Trump's speaking style as below the level of a sixth-grader.[1] The implication was that Trump was simpleminded.

I might have been the first public figure to point out that Trump's simple language was perfect persuasion. Here's why.

Match the speaking style
of your audience. Once
they see you as one of
their own, it will be easier
to lead them.

Trump spoke the way the majority of
voters speak.

Trump's simple speaking style made him
relatable to the average undereducated voter.
This is another example of Trump using pacing
and leading. First you match your audience to
gain their trust. Then you can lead them. This
is powerful persuasion.

SIMPLER LOOKS RIGHT

Our minds are wired to believe that the simplest explanation for events is
probably the correct one. This belief even has a name: Occam's razor. In
the context of science, the simplest explanation that explains your observations is more likely to be right than the one with hundreds of variables
and assumptions. But when you take Occam's razor to the nonscience
world, it quickly becomes nonsense. The reality is that we humans fool
ourselves into thinking that the explanation of the world we hold in our
minds is usually the simplest one. But that is an illusion. Let me give you
some examples to make that point.

If I ask you where life on Earth came from, you might say God did it.
That's the simplest explanation, and billions of people believe it. But a
nonbeliever would not find that so simple. He might ask where God came
from. He might ask why God decided to create a world of creatures he
loved while also making them the food source for each other. Nothing is
ever simple when you dig into it.

Suppose I ask a *non*believer how life formed. He might say evolution
did it. Simple! But that masks a lot of complexity in how DNA mutates,
how species compete and reproduce, how eyeballs formed, and more. My
simple truth might look like a complicated mess to you. And vice versa. It's
subjective.

I used Occam's razor in writing my book *God's Debris*. The main character in that fictional story is written as the smartest person alive. But
since I am not the smartest person alive, and I had to write dialogue for a

character who was, I had a problem. I don't
know what the smartest person in the world
would say! How could I? So I used Occam's razor to create the illusion that the character was
smart. He explained reality in such simple
terms that they register as being persuasive to
the reader. The simplicity itself carries credibility, even though it doesn't earn it.

> **PERSUASION TIP 28**
>
> Simple explanations look
> more credible than
> complicated ones.

MEMORABLE

One of the special features of Trump's speaking style is that it is naturally
viral. The way he words things—especially the simplicity of it—makes
his points easy to remember and easy to repeat. He's a human quote machine. On Twitter his supporters routinely end their tweets with a Trump
catchword: Sad!

As I mentioned earlier in the book, Trump
branded his opponents with easy-to-remember
labels including "crooked," "low-energy," "lying,"
"little," and "goofy." Had he chosen more com-
plex criticisms, we wouldn't quote him, and the
ideas would stay walled off in the garden of in-
tellectual thinkers. But if you call a political
opponent "Fake-tears Schumer," you know it
will go viral. And it did.

> **PERSUASION TIP 29**
>
> Simplicity makes your
> ideas easy to understand,
> easy to remember, and
> easy to spread. You can be
> persuasive only when you
> are also memorable.

STRATEGIC AMBIGUITY

In the early days of the Republican primary season, there were plenty of
Republicans who wanted to support Trump, but their policy preferences
didn't align with his. You can't please the people who want policy X at the
same time as the people who hate policy X. Trump solved that (partly) by
telling everyone what they wanted to hear. It was shamelessly effective
persuasion. Here's how I described it at the time.

Posted March 1, 2016

If you have been watching the news lately, you know that Donald Trump disavowed the endorsement of racist David Duke. Unless you are watching CNN, in which case, their version of the news is that he didn't do enough disavowing that one time.

If you're a racist, you have a reason to like Trump because of CNN's misreporting, and the fact that Trump didn't do enough disavowing that one time. If you're *not* a racist, you can like Trump because he disavowed racists several times, in writing and on video.

That's strategic ambiguity.

If you hate socialized health care, you might like Trump because he hates socialized medicine too. Except that he also says he won't let people with no money "die on the streets." So if you like socialized medicine, you might like giving free health care to those people, like Trump.

That's strategic ambiguity.

If you hate illegal immigrants, you might like Trump because he once said he will deport every one of them. But if you feel compassion for undocumented immigrants who are otherwise good residents of the country, Trump's administration is focusing only on the ones who committed additional crimes after illegally entering the country.

That's strategic ambiguity.

If you oppose war, you might like Trump because he claims he opposed the Iraq war and he says he has a history of being reluctant to commit U.S. forces overseas. But if you think the United States should keep bombing other countries, Trump might be your candidate, because he wants to "bomb the shit out of ISIS" and maybe kill some of their families too.

That's strategic ambiguity.

If you want a religious president, Trump can give you that. He has belonged to a church since youth and he says the Bible is a "great book." But if you don't like mixing religion and politics, Trump might be your candidate, because he hasn't made a big deal about religion.

That's strategic ambiguity.

I could go on like this for another hour or so, but I think you get the picture. And when you see the pattern, you realize none of it is by accident. Trump intentionally gives opposing sides reasons to like him, or at least not disqualify him. And as ridiculous as it seems for a strategy, it works like a charm because of confirmation bias. People see whatever they want to see.

You might be aware that I have been saying good things about Donald Trump's persuasion skills for months. This has led many people to believe I endorse Trump for president.

But earlier this week [Note: This was written in March of 2016] I disavowed Trump for his strategic ambiguity on racism. So if you hate Trump, you can be okay with me because I disavowed him. And if you love Trump, you can be okay with me because I say good things about his talent on a regular basis.

That's strategic ambiguity.

Now you know why I disavowed Trump for not disavowing racism hard enough that one time, even though he clearly disavowed it before and after the time he did not disavow it so clearly. The facts were never important to me. I ignored the facts publicly and shamelessly because doing so provided me the best possible outcome: strategic ambiguity.

PERSUASION TIP 30

"Strategic ambiguity" refers to a deliberate choice of words that allows people to read into your message whatever they want to hear. Or to put it another way, the message intentionally leaves out any part that would be objectionable to anyone. People fill in the gaps with their imagination, and their imagination can be more persuasive than anything you say.

Strategic ambiguity is especially useful when you are trying to persuade lots of people at the same time, and they all have different hot buttons. How will Trump make America great again? The answer: any way you want it to happen. I might imagine that Trump improves the economy, because that's what I care about, while you imagine he defeats ISIS, because you think that is the top priority. With Trump, you get to fill in the blanks with your most potent self-hypnosis.

PART 5

WHY JOINING A TRIBE MAKES YOU POWERFUL AND BLIND

HOW I USED THE PERSUASION FILTER TO PREDICT

As I mentioned earlier in the book, a good filter on reality is one that makes you happy and does a good job of predicting the future. My Persuasion Filter checked both boxes. My followers on Twitter enjoyed my predictions and found them to be downright spooky in their accuracy. I'll describe a few of the fun ones.

PREDICTING THE TOUCHING AND LOVE

Candidate Trump's biggest problem toward the end of the campaign, by far, was that the Clinton team did a great job of branding him as a racist. It was strong persuasion, and it required a well-engineered persuasion response. Visual persuasion is the only type powerful enough for this situation. As I mentioned in a prior chapter, I suggested (some said predicted) that Trump could solve the racism accusations with some well-chosen visuals. Watch how this idea developed in my blog posts over three months.

Posted April 25, 2016

Trump can prove he's not a racist. That's easy. All he needs to do is hug a bunch of nonwhite folks on camera. Real racists don't hug the ones they dislike. They just don't.

Posted May 6, 2016

I recently blogged that Trump's best strategy against charges of racism would be to hug a lot of nonwhite people in public. Racists can't do that. Racists can lie, but no one is convinced by words in this sort of situation. Actions, on the other hand, are usually unambiguous. If Trump had any trouble kissing nonwhite babies, it would be obvious to all. You can't fake physical affection when the cameras are rolling. Expect more hugging and kissing.

And indeed we did see candidate Trump being openly affectionate with African Americans, especially babies who didn't want any part of it. Now you might say, and fairly so, politicians kiss babies all the time. That's true. But a quick search of Google images will tell you that the photos of Trump kissing black babies happened mostly after my predictions, and after a summer of Clinton hammering Trump on his alleged racist ways. When Clinton started focusing on the racism card during the summer of 2016, Trump's poll numbers started to decline. By election day, Trump ended up getting more African American votes than the prior Republican nominee, Mitt Romney.[1] That isn't a fair comparison because Romney's opponent was Barack Obama. Still, it could have been worse for Trump, and no one would have been surprised.

Posted September 3, 2016

Posted September 25, 2016

Posted October 18, 2016

Does the fact that candidate Trump did exactly what I suggested mean I somehow influenced the campaign? No. In this case it was fairly obvious that creating more photo opportunities with African American voters was a good persuasion strategy. I won't take credit for suggesting an idea that would be obvious to any experienced persuader. The interesting point I'll make here is that you can fit this data to three different filters on reality. It fits the filter that says I was predicting what the Trump campaign would do. It fits the filter that I was influencing the campaign, if that makes you happy. And it fits the filter that I did little more than describe a common political practice. But no matter the filter, it supports my main thesis that Trump knows persuasion and applies it. Persuasion-wise, this was the right play. It was visual persuasion (the best kind), and on point.

PREDICTING THAT TRUMP WOULD BE RUNNING UNOPPOSED

By late 2015 I was predicting that Clinton had undisclosed health issues that would result in Trump "running unopposed" by election day. And I based that prediction on nothing but my skill as a hypnotist to detect "tells" in a person.

Sound crazy?

Researchers believe they can create a bathroom mirror that will detect major health issues by detecting day-to-day changes in your face.[2] And it makes sense that humans would evolve to recognize potential mates with the best health. You know from experience that you can tell when a loved one is sick just by observation. We're all capable of detecting a deathly ill person by appearance alone. Some of us are more observant and can detect smaller signals and lesser illnesses. Doctors, for example, are probably far better than the average person at visually detecting illness in a patient, thanks to both training and experience.

Hypnotists are not doctors, but we do learn to observe small "tells" in a subject's face. And that means we are more likely to notice any small variations from day to day, simply because we are attuned to them. Minor variations in a person's face, from one day to the next, are reliable indicators of a health issue, even if the issue is just stress or a lack of sleep.

What I saw in Hillary Clinton was an unusual degree of *variability* in her appearance that you don't find in healthy people. Some days she looked great. Other days she looked tired, pained, and sickly. Her health appearance was all over the place. Compare that with Trump. He looked the same every time you saw him. That's a sign of good health.

Now consider the audacity of my prediction that Clinton's health would take her out of the race by election day. Has something like that ever happened to a presidential candidate in the final months? There were no medical reports to back up my prediction. It seemed to many observers that I was either crazy or being intentionally provocative. Worse yet, my opinion on Clinton's health was viewed as totally irresponsible because I am not a doctor, and I had no business putting those thoughts in people's heads.

My explanation for my actions at the time was that the Persuasion Filter needed the most rigorous test I could give it in public. I was intentionally predicting the hard-to-predict so I could show the power of persuasion. In any other context, I would agree that people with no medical training should avoid speculation about the health of candidates. But I was doing a public demonstration of persuasion that I believed to be important. And I was also confident about my prediction. Otherwise I wouldn't have mentioned it.

Two months before the election, Clinton lost consciousness at a September 11 memorial event and was captured on video as her Secret Service team dragged her unconscious body into an SUV. The official story from the Clinton camp was that she was dehydrated. Soon afterward, they clarified that the problem was pneumonia. Clinton stayed off the campaign trail for three days before resuming a pared-down schedule appropriate to her energy at the time. In the closing months she didn't even campaign in some states that she (mistakenly) thought were safe wins.

In a literal sense, Trump never ran "unopposed." But my unlikely prediction of a health issue taking Clinton out of the race turned out to be so close to reality that my Twitter followers considered it spooky.

The Persuasion Filter predicts that more information about Clinton's health during the campaign will leak out over time. For her sake, I hope I'm wrong. But if I'm right, you'll want to reread this book.

PREDICTING THE TURN TO "TEAM" INSTEAD OF "TRUMP"

Clinton and her supporters did a great job during the campaign of branding Trump as "divisive." It was good persuasion because Trump kept serving up lots of confirmation bias to support their claim. Anytime he talked tough, his opponents labeled him "divisive."

Clinton's Web site included a lengthy article detailing his divisive ways, with this title: "America Deserves Better Than This: Trump's Divisive and Offensive Rhetoric Prove He's Unfit to Be President."

A quick Google search on "Trump divisive" returns *millions* of results. The attack was working. People saw divisiveness in everything Trump did. He made it easy with his provocative rhetoric. It was a big problem, and Trump needed to solve it. In July of 2016, I helpfully posted this.

Posted July 18, 2016

Have you ever noticed that professional sports teams are great at overcoming racism and getting everyone to play together? That's because the coach has persuaded the players to see the *team* as their dominant identity. Trump can do the same with America. Just tell us we're on the same team, and that we're in a *friendly* competition with the rest of the world. I don't care what gender and ethnicity you are, so long as you're with me on the American team and helping to compete against the rest of the world.

The words "Team America" would be the strongest persuasion this country has ever seen. That framing loses the xenophobia and hate, and defines us as part of a friendly competition with the world. The only downside is that *Team America* is the name of a hilarious puppet movie by the creators of *South Park*. But I think we can get past that.

I'm on Team America. If you're on my team, I don't need to know anything else about you. We're good.

By late October, Trump had changed his stump speech to emphasize the word "we." Here are some excerpts from an October 23, 2016, speech:[3]

"*We* are going to bring back the American dream."

"It is gridlock in Washington. Lack of leadership in Washington. And *we* are going to stop it."

"*We* are going to have a dynamic country."

People noticed (and it might have been confirmation bias) that Trump's move to "we" came after my blog on the topic, and they connected what they imagined to be the dots. They wondered on social media if I had influenced the change. I don't claim any influence in this situation because this was a fairly obvious response to the "divisive" branding.

On the other hand, this move had been an obvious way to go for months. And sooner would have been better. The timing of the shift, so soon after my blog post on the topic, was enough to supply confirmation bias to my Twitter followers. To them, it was obvious I had influenced the move. But I don't make that claim. My claim is that trained persuaders think alike. Trump simply did what anyone with his skill set would have done.

PREDICTING BOLTON'S MUSTACHE PROBLEM

After winning the election, President-elect Trump went about the business of filling his cabinet. Normally, cabinet appointments are based on competence, experience, loyalty to the president, and other normal stuff. In the 2-D world, that is all you think you need. But a Master Persuader operating in the third dimension also pays attention to the brand.

Those of us who want to live in a just society don't want a person's appearance to be a job qualification. But you can't change human nature. We are visual creatures, and irrational too. Looks matter, even when we wish they did not. Looks are part of the brand, and Trump was trying to build a brand that people would like. This brings us to John Bolton.

John Bolton was on the short list for secretary of state. He was thoroughly qualified, Republican, and a Trump supporter. Many observers thought he would get the job. But he had two incompatibilities with the brand that Trump was trying to build:

He had an unusual mustache (by the standards of 2017).

He was famously hawkish, meaning he was a proponent of projecting American military power when it was in the national interest.

In a more normal year, neither of those things would be a stopper. But the context in this case was that Trump had been branded as the next Hitler. This is how I explained it at the time in my blog.

Posted December 6, 2016

Bolton would be the biggest brand mistake for Trump. Bolton is highly capable, but he gives off a scary vibe, and that is the worst branding mistake Trump could make. Half of the United States is already living under an illusion that Hitler just got elected president of the United States. If you add a war-loving white guy with a *strange mustache* to the illusion, you're just making things worse. Trump's biggest problem, brandwise, is that so many people think he's a crazy dictator who can't be trusted with the nuclear codes. Bolton is the only candidate who makes that illusion *worse*. I don't see Master Persuader Trump making a mistake of that size.

Trump eventually picked Rex Tillerson for secretary of state. The *Washington Post* reported on December 22, 2016, that according to a Trump insider, Bolton's mustache was likely a factor in the decision.[4] Here's how the *Washington Post* described it.

"Presentation is very important because you're representing America not only on the national stage but also the international stage, depending on the position," said Trump transition spokesman Jason Miller.

Several of Trump's associates said they thought that John R. Bolton's brush-like mustache was one of the factors that handicapped the bombastic former United Nations ambassador in the sweepstakes for secretary of state.

"Donald was not going to like that mustache," said one associate, who spoke on the condition of anonymity to speak frankly. "I can't think of anyone that's really close to Donald that has a beard that he likes."

Technically, my blog about Bolton's mustache was not a prediction. But I did call out a key factor that was invisible to other observers. By then my followers on Twitter and elsewhere were already stunned at what they saw as the accuracy of my Trump-related predictions. When the *Washington Post* confirmed my mustache analysis as valid, brains were exploding all over the Internet. It is one thing to predict a winner in the presidential race—after all, millions of voters and a handful of pundits predicted a Trump win—but this mustache situation seemed to observers like a different level.

Let's remind one another that sometimes a blind squirrel will find a nut. Sometimes that squirrel finds more than one nut. Maybe I just got lucky about the mustache.

Or maybe not.

WHY I ENDORSED
CLINTON (FOR MY SAFETY)
UNTIL I DIDN'T

O ver the course of the presidential campaign I endorsed three candidates. If you're living in the second dimension, you might think I look like a flip-flopper with no core convictions. You have to go to the third dimension to understand why my multiple endorsements worked out the way I intended. But first I'll need to give you some context about my own political history so you know where I'm coming from.

I don't vote. Doing so would destroy whatever objectivity I might have. Once you join a side—for anything—it kicks your confirmation bias into overdrive. Suddenly (and it does happen fast) you start to see everything your side does as wise, while anything happening on the other side looks like stupidity and bad intentions. I minimize that particular confirmation-bias trap by not joining a political side and by not voting.

I have voted in the past. My first vote as a young man was for Jimmy Carter. In time, I came to see that vote as further evidence that the thing I call my common sense is an illusion. (Carter was a good role model but not one of our most effective presidents. He served one term.) As I got older, and more aware of my mental limitations, I came to understand that my vote adds nothing to the quality of the outcome. As far as I can tell, no one else adds intelligence to the election outcome either, but most voters think they do. And that illusion is necessary to support the government. It gives the voters a sense of empowerment and buy-in. That creates national stability. The democracy illusion is probably one of the most beneficial hallucinations humankind has ever concocted. If you think democracy works, and you act as if it works, it *does* work.

I think of democracy as more of a mental condition than a political system. Democracy works because we think it works, and we want it to work. But if you removed the public hallucination that an average ignorant voter has the ability to forecast the future, the whole thing would fall apart.

The democracy illusion is so robust that we can simultaneously know it is absurd while living our lives as if it were not. We all know that the vast majority of our fellow citizens are too underinformed and simpleminded to make good voting decisions. And yet there is widespread acceptance of the majority-vote system. As long as citizens buy into the illusions that they have superpredictive powers and that their votes add intelligence to the system, they will support the democratic voting process that is the foundation of the republic.

If people were rational, they would realize they don't have the psychic powers required to distinguish between a great candidate for president and a bad one. We're terrible at predicting the future. And voters certainly don't understand the more complicated questions about health care, budgets, and international treaties, to name a few. But if we accepted the limitations of our own predictive abilities, we wouldn't vote, and we wouldn't feel as much allegiance to the country, so the whole system would fall apart.

By the way, the Pledge of Allegiance in the United States, and the tradition of singing the national anthem before big events, are examples of government-grade mind control. Those traditions have no other purpose. By the time a child is twelve years old, the state has already trained the kid to sacrifice his or her life for the flag if called to do so.

This is why I don't speak the actual words to either the Pledge of Allegiance or the national anthem. I just move my lips while thinking, *Blah, blah, blah.* It's probably too late to erase my early-life brainwashing, but I see no need to reinforce it. And at this point in my life, I believe (irrationally) that I am a patriot to the bone, so I don't need more brainwashing to be a good citizen.

To be super clear, I am completely in favor of my government brainwashing its citizens, including me. The alternative would involve eventual conquest by a nation that did a better job of brainwashing its citizens.

When I was younger, I believed I could predict who would do a great job as president. But when I compare all my past expectations of new presidents with their actual performance, it is clear that I didn't have any predictive powers. Neither do you. But you might think you do. That's where we differ. If you have not studied persuasion in any detail, you probably hold a higher opinion of your so-called common sense than trained persuaders do.

More disclosure about my voting: I supported Bill Clinton in both of his elections, and I preferred Al Gore over George W. Bush. I can't remember if I bothered to vote in any of those elections. But I haven't voted in any election since.

When Gore narrowly lost to Bush, I was mildly disappointed. But I also thought Bush would be a perfectly good president who wouldn't get the country into any big trouble. Clearly I can't predict who will do a good job as president. Neither can anyone else. But most of us think we can.

To round out my political confessions, I'm super liberal on social matters. If something makes you happy, and it doesn't hurt anyone else, I want you to do a lot of it. On other issues I'm a "whatever works best" kind of guy. And I usually recognize that I don't know what works best on any complicated global issue.

Given all of that, it is no surprise that I started out by endorsing neither Clinton nor Trump for the election of 2016. I enjoyed Trump's personality and his persuasion talents, but my political preferences didn't align with either candidate's stated policies. I was blissfully independent. But that didn't last.

My blogging and tweeting about Trump's persuasion powers made me a Trump supporter by default. I couldn't hide my admiration for his skill set and his entertainment value. And that admiration was enough to activate the bullies and Internet trolls on Clinton's side to come after me. And come after me they did.

The world learned during the election that Clinton's side was spending $1 million on online operatives (more commonly referred to as trolls)

to attack Trump supporters on social media. David Brock, a major Clinton supporter, created an organization called Correct the Record to act as the rabid attack dogs of social media.[1]

The Clinton trolls filled my Twitter feed with personal and professional insults. They tweeted embarrassing fake news stories about me. They wrote to newspapers and asked them to discontinue carrying *Dilbert*. They threatened my reputation and my livelihood in a variety of ways. That stuff didn't bother me. I'm a professional. I know how to deal with critics.

But things got darker. Much darker.

Clinton supporters were doing a good job of branding Trump as Hitler. They did such a good job that perhaps a quarter of the country imagined Trump getting elected and authorizing concentration camps for illegal immigrants on day one. This is the sort of dangerous branding that can get a candidate killed. After all, if you had a chance to kill Hitler and save millions of lives, wouldn't you have a moral obligation to do it?

That's how bad it got. The Hitler accusations evolved from hyperbole to legitimate fear. People were literally afraid of Trump turning full Hitler on inauguration day. It was a dangerous time to be Trump, with that hanging over him. But Trump had Secret Service protection, and apparently they do a great job.

I did not have Secret Service protection. And before long, the Clinton trolls were branding me as Joseph Goebbels, Hitler's propaganda chief. The accusations were repeated often enough to start getting sticky. In my opinion (the only opinion that mattered in this case) it was a dangerous situation. People believed Trump was as bad as Hitler, and by extension that marked his alleged propaganda chief (me) for death as well.

I mean all of this literally. If you have been brainwashed to believe Hitler is coming to power, and you have a chance to kill Goebbels, you have moral authority to do it. If I believed I could kill a top Nazi and slow down Hitler's rise, I would do it in a heartbeat. I assumed other people might feel the same way. It was a dangerous situation for me, and dangerous to any friends and family who might be around me. I decided I needed to do something to reduce the risk.

So I announced my decision to endorse Hillary Clinton, while making it clear I was only doing it for my personal safety. People laughed. They assumed I was joking. But I stuck to my endorsement, mentioning it often, and always appending "for my safety" to the end as an explanation.

I wasn't joking. I was quite serious about trying to lower my risk.

The number of people on Twitter accusing me of being Goebbels slowed to a trickle almost immediately. In the second dimension, that outcome makes no sense. Both sides knew I wasn't serious about being on Clinton's team in the normal way endorsements work. But it didn't matter. People care that you're on their team more than they care why. My stated reason (personal safety) was completely rational, and I backed it with examples of Trump supporters being attacked in my part of the world.

Backing Clinton "for my personal safety" became a running joke on Twitter. My followers enjoyed it, and the trolls were just confused by it. The trolls never left me alone, but they backed off a lot. The endorsement worked exactly as planned. It was solid persuasion.

Here is the blog post announcing my Clinton endorsement.

Posted June 5, 2016

I've decided to come off the sidelines and endorse a candidate for president of the United States.

I'll start by reminding readers that my politics don't align with any of the candidates. My interest in the race has been limited to

Trump's extraordinary persuasion skills. But lately Hillary Clinton has moved into the persuasion game—and away from boring facts and policies—with great success. Let's talk about that.

This past week we saw Clinton pair the idea of President Trump with nuclear disaster, racism, Hitler, the Holocaust, and whatever else makes you tremble in fear.

That is good persuasion if you can pull it off, because fear is a strong motivator. It is also a sharp pivot from Clinton's prior approach of talking about her mastery of policy details, her experience, and her gender. Trump took her so-called woman card and turned it into a liability. So Clinton wisely pivoted. Her new scare tactics are solid-gold persuasion. I wouldn't be surprised if you see Clinton's numbers versus Trump improve in June, at least temporarily, until Trump finds a countermove.

The only downside I can see to the new approach is that it is likely to trigger a race war in the United States. And I would be a top-ten assassination target in that scenario, because once you define Trump as Hitler, you also give citizens moral permission to kill him. And obviously it would be okay to kill anyone who actively supports a genocidal dictator, including anyone who wrote about his persuasion skills in positive terms. (I'm called an "apologist" on Twitter, or sometimes just "Joseph Goebbels.")

If Clinton successfully pairs Trump with Hitler in your mind—as she is doing—and loses anyway, about a quarter of the country will think it is morally justified to assassinate its own leader. I too would feel that way if an *actual* Hitler came to power in this country. I would join the resistance and try to remove the Hitler-like leader. You should do the same. No one wants an *actual* President Hitler.

So I've decided to endorse Hillary Clinton for president, for my personal safety. Trump supporters don't have any bad feelings about patriotic Americans such as me, so I'll be safe from that crowd. But Clinton supporters have convinced me—and here I am being 100 percent serious—that my safety is at risk if I am seen as supportive of Trump. So I'm taking the safe way out and endorsing Hillary Clinton for president.

As I have often said, I have no psychic powers and I don't know which candidate would be the best president. But I do know which outcome is most likely to get me killed by my fellow citizens. So for safety reasons, I'm on team Clinton.

My *prediction* remains that Trump will win in a landslide based on his superior persuasion skills. But don't blame me for anything President Trump does in office; I endorse Clinton.

The rest of you are on your own. Good luck.

THEN I ENDORSED TRUMP

My Clinton endorsement served me well until late September of 2016, when Clinton announced plans for increasing estate taxes on the rich to what I consider confiscation levels. This was personal. I started life with almost nothing and worked seven days a week for decades to build the wealth I have now. I wasn't in the mood to let the government decide what happens to my money when I die. Below is the blog post in which I explained my switch to endorse Trump.

Keep in mind that endorsing Trump reattracted all the risk I had successfully avoided by endorsing Clinton. But the estate tax plan made me too angry to care. I earned my money through hard work, and I already paid taxes on it. This was personal.

This was also the day I decided to move from observer to persuader. Until then I was happy to simply observe and predict. But once Clinton announced her plans to use government force to rob me on my deathbed, it was war. Persuasion war.

Here's how I blogged it at the time.

Posted September 25, 2016

As most of you know, I had been endorsing Hillary Clinton for president, for my personal safety, because I live in California. It isn't safe to be a Trump supporter where I live. And it's bad for business too. But recently I switched my endorsement to Trump, and I owe you an explanation. So here it goes.

1. **Things I Don't Know:** There are many things I don't know. For example, I don't know the best way to defeat ISIS. Neither do you. I don't know the best way to negotiate trade policies. Neither do you. I don't know the best tax policy to lift all boats. Neither do you. My opinion on abortion is that men should follow the lead of women on that topic because doing so produces the most credible laws. So on most political topics, I don't know enough to make a decision. Neither do you, but you probably think you do.

Given the uncertainty about each candidate—at least in my own mind—I have been saying I am not smart enough to know who would be the best president. That neutrality changed when Clinton proposed raising estate taxes. I understand that issue and I view it as robbery by government.

I'll say more about that, plus some other issues I do understand, below.

2. **Confiscation of Property:** Clinton proposed a new top Estate Tax of 65 percent on people with a net worth over $500 million. Her Web site goes to great length to obscure the actual policy details, including the fact that taxes would increase on lower-value estates as well. See the total lack of transparency here [link omitted for book], where the text simply refers to going back to 2009 rates. It is clear that the intent of the page is to mislead, not inform.

So don't fall for the claim that Clinton has plenty of policy details on her Web site. She does, but it is organized to mislead, not to inform. That's far worse than having no details.

The bottom line is that under Clinton's plan, estate taxes would be higher for anyone with estates over $5 million(ish). I call this a confiscation tax because income taxes have already been paid on this money. In my case, a dollar I earn today will be taxed at about 50 percent by various government entities, collectively. With Clinton's plan, my remaining 50 cents will be taxed again at 50 percent when I die. So the government would take 75 percent of my earnings from now on.

Yes, I can do clever things with trusts to avoid estate taxes. But that is just welfare for lawyers. If the impact of the estate tax is nothing but higher fees for my attorney and hassle for me, that isn't good news either.

You can argue whether an estate tax is fair or unfair, but fairness is an argument for idiots and children. Fairness isn't an objective quality of the universe. I oppose the estate tax because I was born to modest means and worked seven days a week for most of my life to be in my current position. (I'm working today, Sunday, as per usual.) And I don't want to give 75 percent of my earnings to the government. (Would you?)

3. **Party or Wake:** It seems to me that Trump supporters are planning for the world's biggest party on election night, whereas Clinton supporters seem to be preparing for a funeral. I want to be invited to the event that doesn't involve crying and moving to Canada. (This issue isn't my biggest reason.)

4. **Clinton's Health:** To my untrained eyes and ears, Hillary Clinton doesn't look sufficiently healthy—mentally or otherwise—to be leading the country. If you disagree, take a look at the now-famous "Why aren't I 50 points ahead" video clip. [Note: This was the viral

video clip in which a drunken-looking Clinton asked in a deranged voice, "Why aren't I fifty points ahead?"] Likewise, Bill Clinton seems to be in bad shape too, and Hillary wouldn't be much use to the country if she has to take care of a dying husband on the side.

5. **Pacing and Leading:** Trump always takes the extreme position on matters of safety and security for the country, even if those positions are unconstitutional, impractical, evil, or something that the military would refuse to do. Normal people see this as a dangerous situation. Trained persuaders such as I see this as something called *pacing and leading*. Trump "paces" the public–meaning he matches them in their emotional state. He does that with his extreme responses on immigration, fighting ISIS, stop-and-frisk, etc. Once Trump has established himself as the biggest badass on the topic, he is free to "lead," which we see him do by softening his deportation stand, limiting his stop-and-frisk comment to Chicago, reversing his first answer on penalties for abortion, and so on. If you are not trained in persuasion, Trump looks scary. If you understand pacing and leading, you might see him as the safest candidate who has ever gotten this close to the presidency. That's how I see him.

So when Clinton supporters ask me how I could support a "fascist," the answer is that he isn't one. Clinton's team, with the help of Godzilla, have effectively persuaded the public to see Trump as scary. The persuasion works because Trump's "pacing" system is not obvious to the public. They see his "first offers" as evidence of evil. They are not. They are technique.

And being chummy with Putin is more likely to keep us safe, whether you find that distasteful or not. Clinton wants to insult Putin into doing what we want. That approach seems dangerous as hell to me.

6. **Persuasion:** Economies are driven by psychology. If you expect things to go well tomorrow, you invest today, which *causes* things

to go well tomorrow, as long as others are doing the same. The best kind of president for managing the psychology of citizens—and therefore the economy—is a trained persuader. You can call that persuader a con man, a snake oil salesman, a carnival barker, or full of shit. It's all persuasion. And Trump simply does it better than I have ever seen anyone do it.

The battle with ISIS is also a persuasion problem. The entire purpose of military action against ISIS is to persuade them to stop, not to kill every single one of them. We need military-grade persuasion to get at the root of the problem. Trump understands persuasion, so he is likely to put more emphasis in that area.

Most of the job of president is persuasion. Presidents don't need to understand policy minutiae. They need to listen to experts and then help sell the best expert solutions to the public. Trump sells better than anyone you have ever seen, even if you haven't personally bought into him yet. You can't deny his persuasion talents that have gotten him this far.

In summary, I don't understand the policy details and implications of the bulk of either Trump's or Clinton's proposed ideas. Neither do you. But I do understand persuasion. I also understand when the government is planning to confiscate the majority of my assets. And I can also distinguish between a deeply unhealthy person and a healthy person, even though I have no medical training. (So can you.)

As you might expect, Trump supporters were happy to see me endorse their candidate. I was all in. I was on the Trump team now, for better or worse.

It didn't take long for *worse* to happen. And you can't get much worse than what happened next.

WHY I BRIEFLY ENDORSED GARY JOHNSON

On October 7, 2016, the *Washington Post* broke the story of a lewd private conversation between Trump and *Access Hollywood* host Billy Bush, caught on a hot microphone. It was devastating.

Persuasion-wise, this had everything. It had audio. It had video. It had sex. It had shock. It was relevant. And it was powerful. As soon as I heard the audio clip, I realized it was a bad idea to associate my brand with Trump. When the scandal broke, Trump was instantly toxic, bordering on radioactive. As women came forward with claims of unwanted advances, I decided to put some distance between Trump's problems and my blogging.

I had already tainted my reputation quite a bit by endorsing Trump. I had trashed my income at the same time, as my speaking career went from thriving to zero. I thought I knew what I was getting into. But I didn't see the so-called Pussygate scandal coming, with its full audio and visual persuasion. This stain wasn't going to wear off. It looked like the end for Trump. The Persuasion Filter can't predict scandals that come out of nowhere.

I decided to put some distance between my brand and Trump's. And so I endorsed third-party candidate Gary Johnson for president. The reason I offered was that Gary Johnson is the kind of candidate who touches only himself. Here's how I explained it at the time.

Posted October 9, 2016

I don't know how to write this post without unintentionally disrespecting the real victims of abuse in any form. I apologize in advance if it comes off that way. But it's part of the national conversation now, and unavoidable. The best I can do is focus on how voters perceive the situation. I don't have an opinion about who did what to whom because I wasn't in the room any of those times. That said . . .

We fine citizens of the United States find ourselves playing some sort of sex-abuse poker in which we have to assign value to various alleged sex crimes to see which alleged rapist/groper/enabler combination we want to inhabit the White House and represent our national brand. Let's call that situation "not ideal."

My view is that if either Clinton or Trump can be judged by the weight of the allegations against them, both are 100 percent unfit for the office. I think Trump supporters think it's worth the hit to our national brand just to get some specific improvements in the country.

Clinton supporters have been telling me for a few days that any visible support for Trump makes you a supporter of sex abuse. From a persuasion standpoint, that actually makes sense. If people see it that way, that's the reality you have to deal with. I choose to not be part of that reality, so I moved my endorsement to Gary Johnson.

I encourage all Clinton supporters to do the same, and for the same reason. I don't know if any of the allegations against the Clintons are true, but since we are judging one another on associations, you don't want to be seen as supporting sex abuse by putting an alleged duo of abusers (the perp and the cleanup crew) into office. I think you will agree that it doesn't matter if any of the allegations are true, because the stink from a mountain of allegations—many that seem credible to observers—is bad for the national brand too. To even consider putting the Clintons back in the White House is an insult to women and every survivor of abuse.

To be fair, Gary Johnson is a pothead who didn't know what Aleppo was. [Note: A reporter asked Johnson about Aleppo, a hot spot in the Syrian conflict, and Johnson didn't recognize the name of the city.] I call that relatable. A President Gary Johnson administration might bring with it some operational risks, and policy risks, but at least he won't slime you by association and turn you into some sort of cheerleader for sex abuse in the way you would if you voted for the Clintons or Trump.

If you take allegations of sex abuse seriously—and you should—vote Johnson. To vote for Clinton or Trump is to be seen by others as an enabler of sexual abuse. I don't think that's what anyone had in mind by breaking the glass ceiling. Don't let it happen to you.

At this point in our story, with only a few weeks before the election, I had lost confidence in my prediction of a Trump win. It seemed that my future would involve losing whatever credibility I had and becoming a laughingstock for years. If history can be our guide, I knew it would take ten minutes for some stranger to update my *Wikipedia* page so the world would forever know just how wrong I had been, with dates and details and links to unflattering articles about me that would be written by the winning pundits.

Things didn't look good for me. Things looked worse for Trump.

Any person with a normal sense of embarrassment would have reversed his prediction to match the pollsters and the experts. That person would have disavowed Trump in a public way. There was still time to salvage some scraps of dignity.

That's not how I played it.

WHY I RE-ENDORSED TRUMP IN THE END

"We got cocky and became arrogant and we also became bullies."

—Actress Zoe Saldana, one week before President Trump's
inauguration in January 2017

I live in northern California, a short drive from Berkeley. It's a liberal place. Trump didn't even bother to campaign in California beyond the minimum. In normal years it is uncomfortable to be a Republican supporter of any type living in northern California. But this was no normal year.

Clinton's team did a great job of framing Trump as a dangerous and unstable Hitler-in-the-making. As I noted before, that provided moral cover for her supporters to threaten and *physically* assault Trump supporters in public.

I'll pause here to stipulate that Trump supporters also caused some trouble. But we learned that much of what was reported as Trump supporters starting trouble turned out to be outright hoaxes, or fights instigated by paid Clinton operatives.

There was the undercover video by Project Veritas that featured Clinton operatives bragging about instigating violence at Trump rallies.[2]

There was the arson of what the media called a "historic black church" that was reported as a suspected hate crime perpetrated by Trump supporters. The real perpetrator turned out to be an African American member of the church.[3]

There was the Muslim woman who claimed she was accosted on a subway by three Trump supporters, but it turned out to be a lie.[4]

We don't need to compare assault rates to know that some Clinton supporters and some Trump supporters crossed the line. Let's agree to not make it a competition. Every large group includes some bad people.

For me personally, Trump supporters were not dangerous because they considered me to be on their side. And I saw no signs of them starting fights with people who were minding their own business. Clinton supporters were another story, and we knew by then that they could be violent. Some examples:

At a Trump rally in San Jose (a short drive from my home), Clinton supporters physically attacked Trump supporters leaving the rally.[5]

Trump supporters were attacked after a Richmond rally.[6]

A Trump supporter was attacked outside a Burlingame rally.[7]

On election day a female Trump supporter was attacked at a Florida polling station.[8]

The mainstream media appeared to be largely ignoring these attacks. But that might have been my own confirmation bias. It didn't take too many similar-looking acts of violence to convince me that there was a pattern here, and a real danger that could get worse.

On Twitter—the Wild West of social media—the bullying from Clinton supporters was relentless. They insulted my appearance, my intelligence, my age, my sexual prowess, my relationships, my height, my baldness—you name it. If it was evil, someone said it to me that year. Probably more than once.

I have a hot button that makes me irrational when I see or experience bullying. I probably could have lived with the bullying and threats if I had been the only target. But Trump supporters all over the country were being assaulted. I heard dozens of stories from victims. I heard stories of people losing customers, losing jobs, being taunted and attacked in public, and having their cars and homes vandalized. This was not politics. This was bully behavior, simple and plain. And it flipped a bit in my brain that I couldn't flip back.

Like many of you, I had some bully issues when I was a kid. I solved my bully problems through a prudent application of public violence, as was the custom in those days in small towns. Oddly enough, I didn't go to jail. That was also the custom in those days. Attacking a bully in a public place wasn't considered bad behavior. It was considered the solution to the problem. That upbringing is still in me.

Summary: I don't like bullies.

Trump was in a huge hole with the *Access Hollywood* scandal, and it got worse with the parade of women who came forward to make claims against him. It seemed that the bullies were going to win. That situation was unbearable to me.

If any anti-Trumpers are reading this book, you are probably scoffing because you consider Trump the only bully in the story. That point of view is what I call word-thinking. But for our purposes here, I'll simply say Trump wasn't bullying *me*. And he wasn't bullying any American citizens who were minding their own business. But he sure did go hard at any opponents who were foolish enough to get into the cage fight with him. I think it makes a difference *whom* you are bullying. I wasn't alarmed when Trump went hard at professional critics. But when someone comes for me personally, or for other citizens, the small-town reflex in me takes over.

I already had a problem with Hillary Clinton trying to rob my estate after I died. Now I also wanted to destroy the entire Democratic Party and all of its "politically correct" Nazi-labeling bullies. I rarely use my persuasion skills at full strength. I only do so in the context of a fight, or for some greater good. This was both.

You need not remind me that Trump supporters on the Internet were also terrible bullies in many cases. But this is *my* story, and they weren't coming after *me*. They were mostly coming after the Clinton bullies, who considered Trump supporters to have less value than other classes of people. I wasn't comfortable with the bullying on either side. But I cared more about the bullies who were coming after me.

On October 25, 2016, I re-endorsed Donald Trump for president of the United States. He has his flaws. But he wasn't bullying *me* and he wasn't trying to rob my estate. By now my lucrative speaking career had dropped from one or two offers per week to zero. In twenty years, that had never happened. My Trump association had gutted a major part of my income and turned me into a pariah. By election day I had lost 75 percent of my so-called friends, several of whom turned out to be bullies too.

As a trained persuader, I prefer not to join any kind of tribe. Doing so triggers an automatic bias toward tribe opinion and blinds one to better thinking. It also marks you as an enemy to competing tribes. Candidate Trump probably got some political advantage by once being a Democrat, later a Republican, and only barely a conservative. He was clearly in the Republican tribe for political purposes, but in our minds he was more like an individual force of nature than a member of a tribe. Our collective impression of Trump's independent thinking probably made it easier for some people to cross party lines and support him. If you want to see the world more clearly, avoid joining a tribe. But if you are going to war, leave your clear thinking behind and join a tribe. Trump joined the Republican tribe to win the presidency. Now I was joining the Trump tribe.

For a war against Hillbullies.

I was all in.

THE THIRD ACT

I was one of the most optimistic of all the pro-Trump public figures. And even I hit bottom after hearing Trump's "grab them by the pussy" comment. I was out of the country when it all went down, and not paying attention to the news. When I finally checked my phone, my Twitter feed was lighting up. I could see the frenzy before I knew what it was about. All I knew was that it was some kind of bad news for candidate Trump, and his supporters were asking me to reassure them he could still win.

No problem, I figured. *Trump gets in trouble once a week. Then he gets out of it.* I had seen it so many times that it seemed routine. And so this new scandal—whatever it was—would surely be more of the same. The cryptic mentions on Twitter referred to some sort of audio recording of Trump saying inappropriate things about women.

How bad could it be?

No problem, I figured. *Trump says five inappropriate things before breakfast. Surely this is no big deal.* By this point in the election story, I had taught my Twitter followers to distinguish a big deal from a little deal, at least in terms of persuasion. I was a bit miffed that—as far as I could tell—they had forgotten how to do it. I figured I would click on the link that everyone was frantically sending me, read it, put it in context, and tell the world via my blog post that it was no big deal, as I had done so many times in the past year.

I clicked the link. I listened to the audio.

I felt my stomach fall through the floor.

Trump was finished, or so it seemed. And so was I. I figured he would go on to enjoy the fabulous life of a billionaire grandfather, and I would live under a cloud of Trump-related humiliation for the rest of my life. This sort of conspicuous failure doesn't wash off. It seemed to be the worst-case scenario.

As you already know, I rapidly switched my endorsement from Trump to Gary Johnson, just to stay out of the blast zone.

But this is where things get interesting. And by "interesting" I mean spooky.

I had been predicting in my blog since the autumn of 2015 that Trump would end up following a classic three-act movie structure before winning. The three-act form looks like this:

First Act: The hero experiences something life changing. In Trump's case, it meant running for president and getting an early lead.

Second Act: In the second act we see the hero having fun, and usually winning, with one minor adventure after another. We watched Trump romp through the Republican primaries, overcoming one obstacle after another, in a surprising and entertaining fashion, just like a proper movie.

The first and second acts often hint at a major problem to come. Trump had overcome one scandalous accusation after another, as you would expect in a second act. But you also had to wonder if something big was ahead. Something terrible. Something that even Trump could not escape. It isn't a good movie unless that happens. And when it comes, we call it the third act.

Third Act: The third and final act is characterized by an impossible-to-solve problem that the hero manages to solve anyway. But don't be fooled by the "fake third acts" earlier in the movie. In the first and second acts, the hero also has hard-to-solve problems. But they pale in comparison with the real third-act problem.

If the movie is written well, the audience will be fooled into thinking that at least one of the second-act problems is really the big third-act problem. For example, it looked as though Trump might be toast after his slow denial of the KKK on CNN, which he attributed to a faulty audio connection. And it looked as if he might be finished when he got tricked into allegedly "insulting" the Khans, the parents of a fallen hero, after their participation in the Democratic convention. In hindsight, those hiccups look like fake third acts.

The "real" third act was the *Access Hollywood* audio leak. No one survives that kind of scandal. Not even Trump. Especially when election day is only a month away. Trump was in an impossible spot. Polls said he had something like a 2 percent chance of winning before the scandal even broke.

By the time Pussygate became the headline story, I had on many occasions discussed my three-act-movie prediction, both on social media and in my blog. That prediction didn't get a lot of attention because it was frankly weird. I offered no basis for my prediction, teasing my social media followers that I would reveal the secret behind the prediction right after the third act happened and Trump won the election. After the win, I explained it this way on my blog.

Posted November 9, 2016

How did I predict the election would turn out so movie perfect? I saw the following situation developing:

1. The social bullying coming from Clinton's supporters guaranteed that lots of Trump supporters were in hiding. That created the potential for a surprise result, so long as the race was close.

2. Trump's powers of persuasion are better than I have ever seen from a living human. That made it likely that the election would be

close. And people generally vote for their party's candidate, so that too promised a close election.

3. The mainstream media backed Clinton. That created a situation in which she was likely to be ahead at some point near the end of the election cycle.

4. The business model of the news industry guarantees lots of "scandals" on a regular schedule. Small things get inflated to big things, and I assumed there would be plenty of them. Trump has the skill to overcome medium-sized scandals and bumps in the road. That's all you need for an entertaining second act.

5. Once I framed this election as a movie script, it primed you to see events that way. Our brains are movie-trained to recognize the three-act form. That's why all movies use it.

That's how I explained my three-act-movie prediction at the time. But it wasn't a complete answer. I saved the spooky parts for this book. But first I have to put it in context.

Keep in mind that my main point of this book is that humans do not see reality as it exists. We didn't evolve to have that capability. What we do have is the ability to rationalize our observations and wrap them into little movies about reality that we create in our minds.

Remember also that there is no way to know if any of our movies is the "right" one, if such a thing even exists. All we can know for sure is that the filter we pick for reality makes us happy, or it doesn't, and it predicts the future well, or it doesn't. That's all we know.

According to the Persuasion Filter, several movies could be running at the same time, on the same screen, and doing good jobs of keeping their viewers happy and predicting what happens next. But what if several completely different movies all had the same ending? Would that mean something?

I have been seeing the world in this multiple-movie way for many years. When Trump started getting traction in the election, several movies popped into my mind. But here's the spooky part.

They were all different movies except for the endings: *Trump won in every movie.*

And that was unusual.

I'll summarize the crazy (perhaps literally) movies I was watching in my head.

The Scott's-Destiny Movie: One of the movies in my head has a spooky script in which I sometimes literally see the future. These "visions," for lack of a less magical-sounding word, happen while I am awake, arrive on their own schedule, and don't fade in memory the way dreams do. In fact, they get stronger over time. And they have a distinct character that feels like neither memory nor imagination. I thought they were just my imagination until I started noticing them coming true. (Yes, each case might have been confirmation bias on my part. That doesn't matter to this point.) I'll tell you about a few of my so-called visions, just to give you an idea what that movie looks like.

When I was about six years old, I saw myself becoming a world-famous cartoonist. It didn't feel like wishful thinking. It felt like something else. My experience of it was that I could see my fate. And it played out pretty much the way I saw it when I was six. I don't have to tell you how rare it is to become a famous cartoonist.

One day in college, I suddenly awoke from a sound sleep with my head full of visions of San Francisco, a place in which I had no family and no connections and for which I had no special affection. A year later, I was living in San Francisco, thanks to at least three unrelated coincidences. I still live in the Bay Area.

On another day in college, I awoke with a vision of myself onstage giving a speech to an indoor crowd of thousands. Years later, I became one of the highest-paid professional speakers in the country, talking to packed ballrooms and theaters all over the country. At the time of the vision, I had no ambitions of being on an actual stage for any reason whatsoever. The idea seemed to come from nowhere.

Those are the so-called visions I can tell you about. I've had this sensation of seeing glimpses of the future perhaps a dozen times. And my unreliable memory tells me each of them came true except for one scheduled for the upcoming five years. Inhabitants of the 2-D world will be quick to note that the most likely explanation of this phenomenon is that I'm lying, or I have selective memory. Those movies are playing on the same screen as my movie, and I don't disparage them. But all of the movies I was watching showed Donald J. Trump becoming president of the United States, against all odds. I could see that future as clearly as my own hand. That doesn't mean I was *really* seeing the future. I don't believe people can see the future. I'm just telling you my subjective experience of it.

By the way, I have in the past made plenty of wrong predictions about all sorts of things. But in those cases, the predictions arose from some combination of 2-D analysis, wishful thinking, and ordinary guessing. My experience of predicting Trump's win was entirely different. My experience of it was that I could "see" it happening in a way that didn't feel like imagination.

To be perfectly clear, if I heard the story I am telling you right now from someone else, I wouldn't believe a word of it. I would assume I was hearing either lies or the result of selective memory. You are welcome to do the same. Remember, I am not presenting this movie as reality, or anything close to it. I'm presenting it as a *rationalization* of my experiences, the same way all of the movies in our heads are formed. If the movie in my head makes me happy, and it predicts the future, that's all I ask of it. This particular movie did make me happy, simply because I find Trump entertaining. And it did predict the future. Good enough.

But this wasn't the only movie in my head that showed Trump winning. There were more. The additional movies are what made this situation spooky.

The Simulated-Reality Movie: In this movie, an earlier species created humans as some sort of software simulation. We believe we are as real as our creators, but there could be billions of simulations for every original species, assuming that every simulation eventually learns to create its own simulations, and so on. In this movie, a lot of computer programming code gets reused for the sake of efficiency, and that's why we see patterns in life where none should exist. In this Trump movie, we are seeing code reuse.

When I noticed that Trump's first act in the primaries was turning into a second act, it made me wonder if this was a case of code reuse in a simulated universe. The three-act-movie form is one of our most common patterns. Trump's first and second acts were so movie perfect that my mind reflexively filled in the third act with his win. This filter on reality assumes that the three-act-movie structure not only happens in our scripted entertainment but is also a recurring pattern that we see in our lives in general. It's a satisfying pattern because it predicts that the hero will come from behind to win.

I'll remind you that I'm not selling this version of reality as true. It is just one of many filters on the world that has the capacity to make me happy. And as you can see, it did a good job of predicting the future in this case.

The Scott-Persuasion Movie: In this movie, I caused Trump's election through my own powers of persuasion. This movie made me happy because I was the hero of it (or the villain if you are a Clinton supporter), and it did a good job of predicting too. I don't hold this movie to be true. It just happens to fit the observed data, exactly like all of the other movies.

The Master-Persuader Movie: In this movie, Trump's world-class persuasion talents take everyone by surprise. In this script, I am an observer who chronicles Trump's persuasion moves, almost like a narrator. This movie became my primary filter on the election, and I thoroughly enjoyed watching it for over a year. The script made me happy, and it predicted a Trump win.

The Bully Movie: In this movie, the so-called social justice warriors supporting Clinton are the bullies who don't know they are bullies. If you have ever seen a movie about a bully, you know the bully has to lose in the end. I love a good bully movie where the victims rise up and prevail against all odds. That sort of story makes me happy. And this movie plot also predicted Trump's win.

As I am sure you know, millions of people were watching a different movie in which Trump was the only bully in the story. I doubt that movie made anyone happy, especially after he won. And it certainly didn't predict well.

The Scott-Wins-from-Behind Movie: I have a wonderful recurring pattern in my life that involves coming from behind to win in a variety of situations. It seems to happen to me with surprising regularity in sports, board games, business, and lots of other realms. You don't need to tell me this is a case of selective memory because that's what it feels like to me as well. The net effect of this observed or imagined pattern is the sense that no matter how deep the hole, I'll win in the end.

Like most people, I've failed at lots of things. I wrote a whole book about my many failures. But the failures rarely involved getting any serious traction in the first place. The coming-from-behind pattern has been limited to situations in which I'm well into the game but behind the leaders.

When election day came, my win-from-behind movie came to dominate my mind as I watched the news coverage of the results. I was supposed to lose to the other pundits who had predicted a solid Clinton win. The pollsters said I was going to lose. My optimism had for a time taken a serious beating by Pussygate. On Twitter, my harshest critics left messages gloating in advance at the humiliating defeat they expected me to experience. Several said they were looking forward to watching me drown in my tears after the election. They promised to visit my Twitter feed for that pleasure alone. It was the perfect movie setup for me to come from behind and win.

And then I did.

WAS I PREDICTING
OR CAUSING?

When you are first exposed to the idea of "filters" on reality, it can be hard to fully embrace the idea. The most challenging part is acknowledging that the human mind is not equipped to understand reality in any deep way. Instead, we create little movies in our minds, and we live in those movies until events in the observable world make that impossible. When our current movie fails, we subconsciously call for a mental rewrite of the script, and our movie changes to fit the observed facts. In this chapter I'll describe a fun example in which two filters explain the same observations. Once you start to recognize this phenomenon, you'll see it all over. I'll prime you with this example.

One of the most interesting questions about Trump's "unexpected" election victory is whether I was simply predicting it or actually causing it (in some small way) with my own persuasion. I realize it sounds absurd to think I was manipulating world events just by typing on my laptop in my kitchen, as I am right now. But let me make the case for it anyway, just so you can see how easily two different filters can describe the same observations.

The only reason I mention the Scott-caused-it filter at all is because my Twitter and blog followers started to wonder if I was doing more than predicting. They wondered if I was actively working for the campaign because it seemed to them that Trump kept making the moves I was predicting. For example, when Trump was being accused of being a heartless monster, I suggested in my blog that he should do something compassionate on camera. I admit this was an obvious move. But it hadn't been done yet, and it had been obvious for some time. The very next day, candidate Trump went into the audience to get personal and touchy with a wounded veteran. The video went viral on social media. My Twitter followers wondered if the timing was a coincidence.

When Clinton secured the Democratic nomination and started painting Trump as a racist, I blogged that the most persuasive defense to that charge was to be physically affectionate with African Americans on camera. A real racist can't fake physical affection and wouldn't even try.

As I mentioned in an earlier chapter, twenty-four hours after writing that blog post, I started getting excited tweets from people saying versions of "He's doing it! He's touching black people on camera!" And so he was. He was kissing a black baby, hugging black adults, and generally being physically affectionate. It wasn't enough to solve his problem—or even close—but it was a step in the right direction.

Lots of pundits had accurate predictions about the election. A normal distribution of luck guaranteed that someone was going to be more accurate than the average. If you think I got lucky with my Trump-related predictions, and that is all that happened, your filter on reality fits the data perfectly. Someone was going to be right, and you know from experience that such a person was going to later claim he or she had special insight. That's exactly what I did. So did the other pundits who predicted Trump's win. Perhaps we got "lucky" and tried to frame it as skill. That view of the world fits every observable fact.

Likewise, if you think this was a situation of confirmation bias—in which people only *imagined* that my predictions matched reality—and perhaps they were ignoring the misses and overinterpreting the hits—that filter on the situation also fits perfectly.

Now we have four viable filters for our observations. One filter says I simply guessed who would become president and got lucky. Another filter says I wasn't accurate at all, but confirmation bias makes it seem as though I was. The third filter says I was accurately predicting the election because my background in persuasion gave me special insight into the situation. The fourth filter says I was *causing* the election outcome, not predicting it.

The interesting thing is that all four filters fit the observable data. That means you will probably never know which—if any—of those filters is right.

Neither will I.

For fun and education only, let's compare the "lucky guess" filter to the idea that I was *influencing* the election and not simply predicting.

Keep in mind that I'm a trained persuader and a professional writer. Objectively speaking, my opinions will usually be more persuasive than the opinions you see from people with less training. Training makes you better at most skills, and persuasion is no different. I've been training in the combined arts of writing and persuasion for about forty years. You should expect me to be far more persuasive than the average pundit, based on practice alone.

During the election, my blog traffic shot up. I was reaching over 100,000 followers with every tweet and blog post. That's a lot when you consider that not many people pay attention to politics at any deep level, especially early in the race. The 100,000 people who saw my early blog posts about Trump were among the people who cared most about politics. These were the voters who followed every interesting angle. Influencing this group would, in theory, have a multiplier effect as they influenced others. When something I wrote went viral—which happened a number of times—millions of people saw my unique framing of issues. Nearly every major media site contacted me during the election and said it was reading my blog. Usually this was in the context of inviting me for an interview or asking for a quote. But many of the contacts were from people in the news business telling me they were fans of my blog and that my Persuasion Filter on the race was the talk of their office.

In the months before election day I heard reliable reports that some members of the Trump campaign staff were aware of my blogging about their boss. Donald Trump Jr. followed me on Twitter and retweeted my work a few times. Candidate Trump retweeted me once. And Trump supporter Newt Gingrich referred to my blog in a published article. I had become hard to ignore. But I have no way to evaluate my impact on anyone's thinking.

I had an emotional reason to try to influence the election because the Hillbullies had triggered me. I don't like bullies. And being human, I also wanted my prediction to be right. So I had good reasons to want to persuade. I was motivated.

Putting all of this in courtroom terms, I had the motivation to persuade, the opportunity, and the right tools for the job. And on election day, events went in the direction I was persuading.

But none of that means I changed any minds.

It is easy to fit the facts to the past in a way that supports a number of theories. As CNN showed us, and I explained in the Cognitive Dissonance chapter, there were dozens of expert explanations for Trump's win, and all of them fit the observed facts. All I've done is add one more example of how you can fit the observed data to different interpretations of the past. You might wonder how anyone could pick the most accurate explanation out of all of those possibilities.

The answer is that we don't have any reliable way to do that.

But just for fun, I have a little trick I use to trace the impact of my persuasion. The method certainly isn't foolproof, and it is more entertainment than science. But in the interest of painting a complete picture here, I'll tell you how I do it: *I use uncommon words and ideas and see if they enter the public conversation.* If I see my unique wording or uncommon framing

The Simple Psychological Trick to Political Persuasion

Conservatives are more likely to support issues like immigration and Obamacare if the message is "morally reframed" to suit their values.

OLGA KHAZAN | FEB 1, 2017 | SCIENCE

Share   Tweet   ...

TEXT SIZE
− +

suddenly leap into widespread use, that means I probably made a dent in the universe. But you can never rule out coincidence.

For example, early in the election cycle, when most pundits were describing Trump as some kind of evil clown, I was using words such as *persuasion, anchors, hypnosis, framing, and negotiation.* By inauguration day, those words had become common in the political press.

Moments ago I was doing a live stream on Periscope and asked my longtime readers if they thought I was the first public person to bluntly say in 2015 that facts don't matter when it comes to picking a president. My audience on Periscope unanimously agreed that they heard it from me first. And they also agreed that other publications started mimicking my writing with science-based articles about how humans are irrational in their decision making. It turns out that science agrees with hypnotists: Humans only *imagine* that facts matter to our decisions. The reality is that we are inventing our own personal facts to fit the movies playing in our heads.

To be fair, I can't rule out the hypothesis that my readers only *imagined* I was the first writer to loudly declare that the facts wouldn't matter in the election. This could be a case of confirmation bias. And the same applies for the next "tell."

In 2015 I started using the metaphor that Trump was playing three-dimensional chess against two-dimensional players. The third dimension, according to my framing, is persuasion. I hadn't heard anyone use that metaphor for Trump until I did. A year later you would see it used by Trump supporters and critics alike. The critics used it in the negative, as in "I doubt he's playing 4-D chess. We just think he's incompetent." (The critics usually escalated my 3-D to a higher number for sarcastic effect.)

CNN politics   45   CONGRESS   SECURITY   THE NINE   TRUMPMERICA   STATE

already had Democrats on edge. This latest report of the sharing of classified information with the Russians will convince them even more of the necessity of a special prosecutor.

✉ **Option #3: Trump is playing 3-dimensional chess**

It is entirely possible that other writers independently realized that facts don't matter in this election because they witnessed it happening. It is also possible that other writers thought of the 3-D chess metaphor on their own. It is a common way to describe higher-level strategy.

Pulling together all of the clues, we know that I am trained in the ways of persuasion, I had a clear motive to persuade voters, I tried hard to persuade, and I had an open channel via social media to the people I wanted to persuade. We also know the outcome turned out to be the one I tried to create. And you can see signs of my nonstandard language choices entering the national conversation.

But all of that proves nothing. Nor is it compelling circumstantial evidence.

As I keep saying—because repetition of this point is useful—you can force-fit lots of different interpretations to the past, and they all work. I know at least three people who believe they were the key reason Trump won. And they all have strong claims.

The reality is that Trump's victory probably required all the help it could get from every source of luck and talent available. I can say with confidence that I swayed *some* votes because I asked on Twitter how many people decided to vote for Trump because of something I said. Thousands of respondents claimed I was the reason they voted the way they did. The Twitter poll only reached a tiny fraction of the people who were exposed to my Trump persuasion. That means I *might* have moved tens of thousands of votes. Maybe hundreds of thousands. There's no way to know.

But I do know I supplied a lot of what I call "fake because" persuasion. In this case, that means people were already primed to vote for Trump, but they didn't want to commit to it, either mentally or otherwise, because the anti-Trumpers did such a good job of painting Trump as Hitler. My framing of Trump as a Master Persuader and not a dictatorial clown gave people a type of psychological cover—permission, if you will—to vote for Trump. I heard from several dozen people over social media that they used my arguments to defend their choices. On the surface, it looks as if I persuaded them. But the "fake because" can be misleading. If I hadn't provided a good "because" that they could use to justify their votes, they would have chosen some other "because." They would have latched onto whatever was the latest news report and declared that the new information was the last straw that turned them to Trump. The people who were leaning toward Trump but not committing were probably going to commit by election day no matter what. People just needed to find their "fake because" to rationalize it. I provided an acceptable "because" in the form of the Master Persuader concept.

Now let's add some context to my movie. If you really want to know how persuasive I was in the election, it might help to know about my track record for this sort of thing. I can't fully disclose my persuasion projects from the past. All I can tell you is that this isn't the first time a national event went my way. However, there is no way to know how much influence, if any, I had in those cases either. Perhaps I am just good at predicting the winning side. It

> **PERSUASION TIP 31**
>
> If you are trying to get a decision from someone who is on the fence but leaning in your direction, try a "fake because" to give them "permission" to agree with you. The reason you offer doesn't need to be a good one. Any "fake because" will work when people are looking for a reason to move your way.

would look the same to observers. And I wouldn't know the underlying truth either, at least not with certainty.

My best guess about my own persuasion is that I did influence a lot of people to change their votes. But I think the Persuasion Filter also did a good job of predicting events during the election. So I think my actions during the election were a mixture of causing and predicting. I don't know which one explains more of what happened.

At the time of this writing I am trying to influence another national topic: climate science. My framing involves separating the science from the prediction models, and the prediction models from the economic models, and evaluating each of them separately. After all, economics is not science. Economics is more like astrology, at least when you're predicting ten years out.

This framing of climate science is not unique to me, but at this writing almost everyone expressing an opinion on climate change says it is either a looming disaster or nothing to worry about. I'm reframing it as three separate topics: the science, the climate models, and the economic models. If you see that framing become the standard way of looking at climate science by the time you read this book, it might be because of my influence.

But we can't know for sure.

Update: A few months after I wrote this chapter, President Trump pulled out of the Paris climate accord, framing it as an economic decision that is independent from the science. President Trump's critics twitched and stomped their feet for a few weeks, until they realized how hard it was to argue in favor of spending billions of dollars for nearly no reduction in global temperatures. When experts confirmed the high cost and low impact of the agreement, I realized I had just witnessed one of the greatest High-Ground Maneuvers in modern history.

Or I caused it.

It all looks the same.

Bonus: Look for a clue in this tweet that the author of the book *Pre-Suasion*, Robert Cialdini, is familiar with my work.

The use of "Master Persuader" in the ad could be a coincidence. But the author did once tell me he enjoyed reading my blog posts about the election. Does it seem that I persuaded Robert Cialdini, one of the most famous experts on persuasion of all time?

Maybe.

But another movie on the same screen says Cialdini persuaded me to include an ad for his excellent book in my book.

Damn it! He's *good*.

ELECTION NIGHT

November 8, 2016.

I had been living a very public life for the past year—more so than usual. During an election cycle, the media is starving for content, and my Master Persuader idea offered something different to help fill the endless minutes. Producers invited me to explain my thoughts about Trump on cable news shows, national radio, print interviews, podcasts, Twitter, Periscope live streams, and more. My thoughts on the election were being retweeted, reposted, quoted, and flat-out stolen by other authors and pundits. But on election day, all I felt was alone. Before the night was over, I would either be a laughingstock for the rest of my life or an unexpected winner of spooky proportions. One way or another, things were about to change for me, and bigly.

I invited my girlfriend, Kristina Basham, to join me to watch the election results come in. Early in the day, the pollsters and the TV experts with their electoral-map projections reminded me every few minutes that I was about to have a bad night, and maybe a bad future.

I had been telling people by social media since the time of Pussygate that I was sticking with my prediction of a 98 percent chance that Trump would win. And by election day, I had moved my endorsement from Gary Johnson back to Trump. I was all in. And I was in a deep hole, just like Trump. For better or worse, my fate was connected to his. And according to just about everyone on television that night, Trump's fate was not looking good.

But a funny thing happened when Florida started reporting votes: All of the movies in my head were still predicting a Trump win. And my optimism returned in force. At this point, my come-from-behind movie was the most dominant of the competing scripts in my mind. Florida was a must-win state for Trump, and when he pulled ahead in the early vote count, I tweeted a one-letter message to my followers.

L

My Twitter feed lit up with people asking what I meant by that one letter. I didn't respond to the questions. When Florida looked like it would be a Trump win, I tweeted a second letter.

A

Even with Florida coming in for Trump, the experts still predicted a comfortable Clinton victory. I wasn't having any of it. I tweeted another letter.

N

Several of my clever followers on Twitter now had enough clues to solve the puzzle. I had been predicting a Trump "landslide" for a year, against all odds. Now I was spelling it out in real time, as the election unfolded. And I was wa-a-a-a-y over my skis. I wasn't in a mood to die timid that night.

My twitter feed started going crazy. Most of my followers were Trump supporters, and the mainstream media had by then crushed their optimism. When they saw my early optimism about the vote results, their optimism returned too, as some later told me. Remember, I had been pacing them for a year. Now I was leading with my own optimism, and they followed. I had been right about many things that year, and they hoped I had one more good prediction in me. I could almost feel the electricity in their comments.

You know the rest of the story.

Trump won some states he wasn't supposed to win, and I completed my "L-A-N-D-S-L-I-D-E" prediction in one more tweet. Trump lost the popular vote, but he won the Electoral College by a solid margin that his supporters called a "landslide" and his critics called "losing the popular vote."

Maybe Trump won because he campaigned better in the right states. Maybe there were more so-called shy Trump supporters than the experts believed. Maybe Trump won because of any one of CNN's twenty-four listed reasons for his win, published soon afterward. Maybe it was because one of the movies in my head is the "real" one. I will never know.

At about midnight, with Trump's election in the bag, I decided to celebrate by enjoying a large amount of California's finest medical marijuana—legally, I might add. On any normal evening I would not consume so much. But this was no ordinary night. Kristina had headed home, and I was alone with my wonderful movies—all of them, replaying in my head. I slipped into bed and expected to be blissfully asleep in minutes. I had avoided the abyss. I was experiencing pure joy.

My phone rang.

A British voice cheerfully greeted me and announced that it was the BBC calling. I had forgotten that I had agreed to take their call on election night to do a live radio interview about the outcome. This was the call. And my brain was on Jupiter.

I had two choices. I could refuse to do the interview that I had promised I would do, or I could thoroughly embarrass myself to the BBC audience all over the world.

Of course I did the interview. That wasn't even a hard choice.

It was one of the best days of my life.

I should remind you once again that my support for Trump was not about his policies. Much will have transpired by the time you read this book. Perhaps President Trump will go on to do great things. Or maybe not. But no matter where fate leads us, you now have a new filter for viewing your experience of reality.

Welcome to the third dimension.

ACKNOWLEDGMENTS

Thank you to all the "deplorables" who made this book possible. You supported me on social media when the going got tough, and you refused to settle for the status quo. You were fearless, smart, and funny. Many of you asked me to write this book, and I was honored to do so. I hope you like what I did with our story.

Thank you to my prescient publisher, Adrian Zackheim, for knowing how to nudge me in exactly the right ways. Thank you to my brilliant editor, Leah Trouwborst, for helping me turn my raw thoughts into a compelling story. And thank you to Chris Morgan for fact-checking along the way to keep me out of trouble.

Thank you to the many haters who came after me during the 2016 election and after. You energized me. Sometimes art needs an enemy.

Thank you to America, for making all of this fun possible. You were already great, but the best is yet to come.

We're just getting started.

APPENDICES

APPENDICES

APPENDIX A

The Persuasion Reading List

Whenever I write about persuasion, readers ask what else they can read on the topic. So I put together what I call the Persuasion Reading List. I haven't read every book on this list. Some are included because the content fits the topic and includes the sort of lessons I have absorbed through different channels.

BOOKS THAT HELP YOU STOP BELIEVING

The first books on my list will help you to be skeptical about your ability to comprehend reality. If you are already a hard-core skeptic, you can skip these.

An Encyclopedia of Claims, Frauds, and Hoaxes of the Occult and Supernatural (James Randi)

They Got It Wrong: History: All the Facts that Turned Out to Be Myths (Emma Marriott)

THE MOIST ROBOT HYPOTHESIS

The Moist Robot Hypothesis first appears in my book that is listed below. The idea is that humans are biological machines, subject to cause and effect. According to this view, free will is an illusion and humans can be programmed once you understand our user interface.

In this part of the list, I ease you into the notion that humans are mindless robots by showing you how we are influenced by design, habit, emotion, food, and words. Until you accept the moist robot view of the world, it will be hard to use your tools of persuasion effectively.

The Design of Everyday Things (Don Norman)

What Every BODY Is Saying (Joe Navarro)

The Power of Habit: Why We Do What We Do in Life and Business (Charles Duhigg)

Influence (Robert B. Cialdini, PhD)

Pre-Suasion (Robert B. Cialdini, PhD)

Thinking, Fast and Slow (Daniel Kahneman)

Salt Sugar Fat (Michael Moss)

How to Fail at Almost Everything and Still Win Big: Kind of the Story of My Life (Scott Adams)

Free Will (Sam Harris)

Predictably Irrational: The Hidden Forces That Shape Our Decisions (Dan Ariely)

A Random Walk Down Wall Street (Burton G. Malkiel)

The Black Swan (Nassim Nicholas Taleb)

ACTIVE PERSUASION

This part of the list gets into the details of how to influence people. My opinion is that you will not be completely effective with these tools unless you have a full understanding of our moist robot nature, introduced above.

Impossible to Ignore (Dr. Carmen Simon)

Trump: The Art of the Deal (Donald J. Trump with Tony Schwartz)

Win Your Case: How to Present, Persuade, and Prevail—Every Place, Every Time (Gerry Spence)

Awaken the Giant Within: How to Take Immediate Control of Your Mental, Emotional, Physical and Financial Destiny! (Tony Robbins)

How to Win Friends & Influence People (Dale Carnegie) (Better yet, take a Dale Carnegie class near you. It will change your life. Trust me.)

How to Write a Good Advertisement (Victor O. Schwab)

The Secret of Selling Anything (Harry Browne)

The One Sentence Persuasion Course: 27 Words to Make the World Do Your Bidding (Blair Warren)

Reframing: Neuro-Linguistic Programming and the Transformation of Meaning (Richard Bandler and John Grinder) (This is included for completeness. Much of the NLP field has exaggerated claims, but there is some strong reality at the base of it.)

How to Hypnotise Anyone: Confessions of a Rogue Hypnotist (The Rogue Hypnotist) (I have *not* read this book, but based on reviews, it probably gives you a good taste of the topic. Do not expect to be a capable hypnotist after reading a book.)

Hypnosis and Accelerated Learning (Pierre Clement) (This is the flavor of hypnosis I learned in hypnosis class. It comes from Ericksonian hypnosis. See next book on list.)

Speak Ericksonian: Mastering the Hypnotic Methods of Milton Erickson (Richard Nongard and James Hazlerig) (Erickson was the father of modern hypnosis. Any book about his methods would be interesting.)

Google "Persuasion Reading List" to see any updates.

APPENDIX B

How to Be a Better Writer

Good writing is also persuasive writing. People will judge your credibility by the quality of your writing. And you need credibility to persuade.

As you learned in this book, President Trump communicates in a style that is simple, provocative, visual, and quotable. Some of that is probably a natural talent. But it turns out that good writing is one of the easiest things to learn. You're about to become a better writer, and it will be as easy as reading my blog post on the topic from 2007, presented below. This post has been widely shared on the Internet since it first appeared. I recommend rereading it about once a year to keep your mind tuned to good form.

Posted on June 16, 2007

I went from being a bad writer to being a good writer after taking a one-day course in "business writing." I couldn't believe how simple it was. I'll tell you the main tricks here so you don't have to waste a day in class.

Business writing is about clarity and persuasion. The main technique is keeping things simple. Simple writing is persuasive. A good argument in five sentences will sway more people than a brilliant argument in a hundred sentences. Don't fight it.

Simple means getting rid of extra words. Don't write "He was very happy" when you can write "He was happy." You think the word "very" adds something. It doesn't. Prune your sentences.

Humor writing is a lot like business writing. It needs to be simple. The main difference is in the choice of words. For humor, don't say "drink" when you can say "swill."

Your first sentence needs to grab the reader. Go back and read my first sentence in this post. I rewrote it a dozen times. It makes you curious. That's the key.

Write short sentences. Avoid putting multiple thoughts in one sentence. Readers aren't as smart as you'd think.

Learn how brains organize ideas. Readers comprehend "the boy hit the ball" quicker than "the ball was hit by the boy." Both sentences mean the same thing, but it's easier to imagine the actor (the boy) before the action (the hitting). All brains work that way. (Notice I didn't say, "That is the way all brains work"?)

That's it. You just learned 80 percent of the rules of good writing. You're welcome.

_____

APPENDIX C

How to Find Out if You Are a Simulation

I often blog about the idea that we might be computer simulations. If we are simulations, how could we deduce our true nature? I took a run at that question in this blog post of April 27, 2017:

Regular readers of this blog know about philosopher Nick Bostrom's idea that it is far more likely we are simulations created by an advanced species than that we are the original species itself. The reasoning here is that every sufficiently advanced species will create multiple simulations in which the simulated creatures believe they are real. So the odds are high that we are one of the many simulations, not the original species that created them.

But how could you tell?

I have a hypothesis. There should be a difference in how a real species and a simulated species views its own history. The real species would have a real history with full details. The simulation would have something closer to history *on demand*. And by that I mean the history comes into existence only when current circumstances require that history. If we are software simulations, the simulator presumably has resource constraints. That means the simulation would not create every part of the universe just in case it is needed; it would create what is needed on demand. For example, a simulated universe would not contain details about undiscovered planets. Those details would be rendered by the simulation at the time of discovery.

To put this in simpler terms, if we are real, the past influences what we do in the present. But if we are simulations, what we do in the present could be *creating the past.*

For example, here's an article [link omitted for book] describing how quantum physicists have determined that the present creates the past as needed. Freaky, right?

If we are simulations, we should expect to see two additional qualities in the universe as partial confirmation:

1. We should expect that we can't travel past the boundaries of the simulation.

2. We wouldn't be able to observe the basic building blocks of our reality.

Sure enough, we meet both criteria.

We can't travel beyond the edge of the universe without exceeding the speed of light, which is theoretically impossible. That's what you would expect in a simulation. You would have some sort of rule of physics to keep the simulated people from traveling beyond the edges. Here I'm assuming the universe is expanding at the same rate as the light that is traveling in all directions, so we can never catch up to it.

The hypothetical creators of our simulation would also try to prevent us from discovering that we are not made of anything real. And sure enough, when science looks at our basic building blocks at the quantum level, all we have is probability and strangeness.

I have viewed the world as having backward causation (the present creates the past) since I was a young man. In my worldview, an envelope you receive in the mail doesn't have definite contents until it is observed. Up until the moment someone sees the contents, the envelope can contain anything that known history has not yet ruled out. This model of the world explains my observations every bit as well as the idea that the past determines my future.

In a simulated reality, we would expect to see lots of confirmation bias and lots of cognitive dissonance. Do you know why?

It keeps the programming simple for the author of our reality.

If we simulations saw our personal experiences accurately, the author of the simulation would have to make your view of history and mine fit together and be consistent on every variable. That would be massively complicated with billions of simulated humans doing things that create their histories on the fly. The solution to that complexity is to allow the simulated humans to hallucinate that whatever they observe coincidentally fits both their histories and their worldviews. That way the simulation doesn't need to create accurate histories for all the players. We can imagine our own histories as being accurate until events in the present make that impossible. Then, and only then, does the simulation decide on a definite past.

Consider the news this week that a recent discovery suggests humans were in North America 100,000 years earlier than scientists believed. That finding is not yet confirmed, but it still works to make my point. Given that this new finding is not yet confirmed, our human history does not need to be rewritten by the simulation. But if new discoveries confirm that humans were in North America this early, our "real" history comes into existence at the moment our observations make it impossible for any other history to be true. Until then, both histories (and more) exist as probabilities, nothing more.

I assume I got some (or all) of the science wrong in this blog post. The only point I want to defend is the idea that a simulated universe would probably need to create its history based on current events, whereas a "real" universe would have an objective history that never changes.

_____

APPENDIX D

Trump's Many Mistakes

I know from experience that some readers will complain I am too generous about President Trump's talents and I am glossing over his flaws and mistakes. But keep in mind this is not a book about politics. My topic is persuasion, and in that field, Trump does far more right than wrong. I'm not qualified to judge the impact of his policies. I assume some will be better than others. His policies don't often align with my own preferences. Don't look to me to defend Republican politics.

Trump's many "mistakes" can be misleading. For example, he knows that saying provocative and often untrue statements will attract energy—which is good—but it comes with a high cost. You can't evaluate the costs of Trump's persuasion systems independently of the benefits. You have to look at the net.

For example, Trump's unscripted and provocative rally speeches were guaranteed to produce some gaffes—both the real and "fake news" kind—but the gain from being spontaneous and freewheeling probably provided more energy and persuasion advantage than downside. Had he been a more cautious candidate, he might have avoided a number of provocations and gaffes, but he also wouldn't have energized his base. Do you score those gaffes as mistakes, or are they a known and acceptable cost of the persuasion strategy he was using? The economist in me looks at the net gain after all costs and benefits are included. His critics focus on the mistakes, and I mostly agree with their identification of the mistakes, give or take a few "fake news" misinterpretations of what he did.

I mentioned in my chapter on scandals that Trump fumbled on several plays. I'll note them here for completeness. I won't re-explain why these are not the mistakes they were reported to be in the mainstream media. I'll simply agree with his critics that he could have handled these situations better.

KKK slow denial

Khan controversy

Spastic imitation of Serge Kovaleski

Calling Judge Curiel "Mexican"

Facts (He often ignored them.)

Tough talk (He probably took it too far at rallies.)

I'm leaving out President Trump's preelection "mistakes," of which there were many. Trump University is near the top of that list. And talking about grabbing women by the private parts while wearing a hot microphone was clearly a mistake. I don't think the public needed me to point out the obvious there.

I also acknowledge that Trump had a number of notable business failures over his multidecade entrepreneurial career that spanned several industries. But the economist in me says he cleverly managed his risks so his successes would outshine his failures. Most new businesses fail, and nearly every billionaire with a complicated portfolio has losers in the bunch. Trump used a well-designed system for pursuing business success: He transferred risk to others when he could, and he made sure his projects were in separate entities so they could fail without bringing down the whole enterprise. That's how Trump could have bankruptcies in his portfolio and still make money. He only needed the winners to be bigger than the losers over time. And that's what happened. If you are not experienced in business, it would be easy to see the bankruptcies as meaning more than they do.

By far the largest set of mistakes President Trump has made in his lifetime fall into the category of *things he could have done better according to me*. I'll grant you the list is long. But I have the same feeling about nearly every public figure.

NOTES

ABOUT FACTS

1. Nate Silver, "Donald Trump's Six Stages of Doom," *FiveThirtyEight*, May 17, 2016, accessed June 28, 2017, https://fivethirtyeight.com/features/donald-trumps-six-stages-of-doom/.
2. "All False Statements Involving Donald Trump," *PolitiFact*, accessed July 26, 2017, http://www.politifact.com/personalities/donald-trump/statements/byruling/false/.
3. Daniel Oppenheimer, "Hard-to-Read Fonts Promote Better Recall," *Harvard Business Review*, March 2012, accessed July 26, 2017, https://hbr.org/2012/03/hard-to-read-fonts-promote-better-recall.

COGNITIVE DISSONANCE

1. "Cognitive Dissonance," *Wikipedia*, Wikimedia Foundation, June 16, 2017, accessed June 28, 2017, https://en.wikipedia.org/wiki/Cognitive_dissonance.

MASS DELUSIONS

1. G. Adams, *The Specter of Salem: Remembering the Witch Trials in Nineteenth-Century America* (Chicago: University of Chicago Press, 2009).
2. Brad Schwartz, *Broadcast Hysteria: Orson Welles's War of the Worlds and the Art of Fake News* (New York: Farrar, Straus and Giroux, 2015).
3. E. W. Butler et al., *Anatomy of the McMartin Child Molestation Case* (Lanham, MD: United Press of America, 2001).
4. Charles Mackay, *Memoirs of Extraordinary Popular Delusions and the Madness of Crowds*, vol. 1 (London: Richard Bentley, 1841).

THE MAKING OF A HYPNOTIST

1. CNN/ORC International, "CNN/ORC International Poll," CNN.com, October 20, 2015, accessed July 26, 2017, http://i2.cdn.turner.com/cnn/2015/images /10/19/rel11b.-.republicans.pdf.

THE PERSUASION STACK

1. Johanna M. Jarcho, Elliot T. Berkman, and Matthew D. Lieberman, "The Neural Basis of Rationalization: Cognitive Dissonance Reduction During Decision-Making," *Social Cognitive and Affective Neuroscience*, July 12, 2010.
2. Daniela Schiller and David Carmel, "How Free Is Your Will?" *Scientific American*, March 3, 2011; Vadim Cherepanov, Timothy Feddersen, and Alvaro Sandroni, "Rationalization in Decision Making," *Kellogg Insight*, July 1, 2009.
3. *Jimmy Kimmel Live*, "Clinton Supporters Agree with Donald Trump Quotes," YouTube, August 4, 2016, accessed June 28, 2017, https://www.youtube.com /watch?v=IzC-l7tovFk.

GO BIGLY OR GO HOME

1. Eli Stokols and Ben Schreckinger, "How Trump Did It," *Politico*, February 1, 2016, accessed July 26, 2017, http://www.politico.com/magazine/story/2016 /02/how-donald-trump-did-it-213581.

IS PRESIDENT TRUMP A "NATURAL" PERSUADER?

1. Paul Schwartzman, "How Trump Got Religion—and Why His Legendary Minister's Son Now Rejects Him," *Washington Post*, January 21, 2016, accessed July 26, 2017, https://www.washingtonpost.com/lifestyle/how-trump-got-religion—and -why-his-legendary-ministers-son-now-rejects-him/2016/01/21/37bae16e -bb02-11e5-829c-26ffb874a18d_story.html?utm_term=.5589a0e16da6.
2. Donald B. Meyer, *The Positive Thinkers: Religion as Pop Psychology, from Mary Baker Eddy to Oral Roberts* (New York: Pantheon, 1980).

HOW TO DESIGN A LINGUISTIC KILL SHOT

1. Dana Milbank, "The Dangerous Donald," *Washington Post*, March 30, 2016, accessed July 26, 2017, https://www.washingtonpost.com/opinions/dangerous -donald—a-stop-trump-label-that-sticks/2016/03/30/710200d6-f6af-11e5-8b23 -538270a1ca31_story.html?utm_term=.c38d4b7ad3bc.

HOW TO CREATE EFFECTIVE CAMPAIGN SLOGANS AND LOGOS

1. Noam Shpancer, "Red Alert: Science Discovers the Color of Sexual Attraction," *Psychology Today*, January 10, 2013.
2. Matt Flegenheimer, "When Hillary Clinton Tested New Slogans—85 of Them," *New York Times*, October 19, 2016, accessed July 26, 2017, https://www.nytimes.com/2016/10/20/us/politics/hillary-clinton-campaign-slogans.html.
3. Tanya Basu, "Google Parent Company Drops 'Don't Be Evil' Motto," *Time*, October 4, 2015, accessed July 26, 2017, http://time.com/4060575/alphabet-google-dont-be-evil/.

GODZILLA GETS IN THE GAME (OR DOES HE?)

1. Lynn Vavreck, "The Ad That Moved People the Most: Bernie Sanders's 'America,'" *New York Times*, December 30, 2016, accessed July 26, 2017, https://www.nytimes.com/2016/12/30/upshot/the-campaign-ads-that-moved-people-the-most.html.
2. Nate Silver, "National Polls," *FiveThirtyEight*, November 8, 2016, accessed July 26, 2017, https://projects.fivethirtyeight.com/2016-election-forecast/national-polls/.

HOW A TRAINED PERSUADER EVALUATES SCANDALS

1. Marlena Baldacci, "Presidential Candidates Have Long History of Releasing Tax Returns," CNN.com, July 16, 2012, accessed June 28, 2017, http://politicalticker.blogs.cnn.com/2012/07/16/presidential-candidates-have-long-history-of-releasing-tax-returns/.
2. Susan Heitler, "How Contempt Destroys Relationships," *Psychology Today*, March 4, 2013.

A GRAB BAG OF TRUMP'S QUICKEST AND EASIEST PERSUASION TOOLS

1. Justin Wm. Moyer, "Trump's Grammar in Speeches 'Just Below 6th Grade Level,' Study Finds," *Washington Post*, March 18, 2016, accessed July 26, 2017, https://www.washingtonpost.com/news/morning-mix/wp/2016/03/18/trumps-grammar-in-speeches-just-below-6th-grade-level-study-finds/?utm_term=.2fc678ccf049; Jack Shafer, "Donald Trump Talks Like a Third-Grader," *Politico*, August 13, 2015, accessed June 28, 2017, http://www.politico.com/magazine/story/2015/08/donald-trump-talks-like-a-third-grader-121340.

HOW I USED THE PERSUASION FILTER TO PREDICT

1. Amanda Sakuma, "Trump Did Better with Blacks, Hispanics Than Romney in '12: Exit Polls," NBCNews.com, November 9, 2016, accessed July 26, 2017, http://www.nbcnews.com/storyline/2016-election-day/trump-did-better-blacks-hispanics-romney-12-exit-polls-n681386.
2. Carl Engelking, "'Smart Mirror' Could Scan Your Face to Detect Health Risks," *D-brief, Discover*, July 28, 2015, accessed July 26, 2017, http://blogs.discovermagazine.com/d-brief/2015/07/28/smart-mirror/#.WXkRWhUrKUk.
3. Lynn Vavreck, "The Ad That Moved People the Most: Bernie Sanders's 'America'," *New York Times*, December 30, 2016.
4. Philip Rucker and Karen Tumulty, "Donald Trump Is Holding a Government Casting Call. He's Seeking 'the Look,'" *Washington Post*, December 22, 2016, accessed July 26, 2017, https://www.washingtonpost.com/politics/donald-trump-is-holding-a-government-casting-call-hes-seeking-the-look/2016/12/21/703ae8a4-c795-11e6-bf4b-2c064d32a4bf_story.html?utm_term=.a7122108637c.

WHY I ENDORSED CLINTON (FOR MY SAFETY) UNTIL I DIDN'T

1. Evan Halper, "Be Nice to Hillary Clinton Online—or Risk a Confrontation with Her Super PAC," *Los Angeles Times*, May 9, 2016, accessed July 26, 2017, http://www.latimes.com/politics/la-na-clinton-digital-trolling-20160506-snap-htmlstory.html.
2. Project Veritas, "DNC Schemes to Bully Women at Trump Rally," YouTube, October 19, 2016, accessed June 28, 2017, https://www.youtube.com/watch?v=b24Yq1Ndnjo.
3. Katie Mettler, "Miss. Black Church Fire Was Called a Hate Crime; Now Parishioner Has Been Arrested for It," *Washington Post*, December 22, 2016, accessed July 26, 2017, https://www.washingtonpost.com/news/morning-mix/wp/2016/12/22/miss-black-church-fire-another-highly-publicized-suspected-hate-crime-debunked-police-say/?utm_term=.c64fd8a34525.
4. Derek Hawkins, "She Claimed She Was Attacked by Men Who Yelled 'Trump' and Grabbed Her Hijab; Police Say She Lied," *Washington Post*, December 15, 2016, accessed July 26, 2017, https://www.washingtonpost.com/news/morning-mix/wp/2016/12/15/she-claimed-she-was-attacked-by-men-who-yelled-trump-and-grabbed-her-hijab-police-say-she-lied/?utm_term=.5c8d718cf247.
5. *Inside Edition*, "Were Donald Trump Supporters Being Hunted Down Like Prey by Protesters?" YouTube, June 3, 2016, accessed June 28, 2017, https://www.youtube.com/watch?v=uWIMt9JxugQ.

6. Alex Jones Channel, "Trump Supporters Attacked at Richmond Rally," YouTube, June 10, 2016, accessed June 28, 2017, https://www.youtube.com/watch?v=9T4 J1EQ-Js8.
7. KTVU, "Raw Video: Donald Trump Supporter Walks Through Angry Crowd of Protesters," YouTube, April 29, 2016, accessed June 28, 2017, https://www.you tube.com/watch?v=4JWw8cTEN14.
8. Christian Datoc, "Female Trump Supporter Attacked by Male Clinton Supporter at Florida Polling Station," *Elections*, *Daily Caller*, November 8, 2016, accessed June 28, 2017, http://dailycaller.com/2016/11/08/female-trump-supporter -attacked-by-male-clinton-supporter-at-florida-polling-station-video/.

INDEX

Also by Scott Adams

Blasting clichéd career advice, the contrarian pundit and creator of *Dilbert* recounts the humorous ups and downs of his career, suggesting you replace unsatisfying goals with systems, dramatically improving your odds of success.

PORTFOLIO PENGUIN | Penguin Random House